W9-CAS-747

ESTHER
A Woman for Such a Time as This

BIBLE STUDY GUIDE

From the Bible-teaching ministry of

Charles R. Swindoll

INSIGHT FOR LIVING

Charles R. Swindoll is a graduate of Dallas Theological Seminary and has served in pastorates in Texas, Massachusetts, and California since 1963. He has served as senior pastor of the First Evangelical Free Church of Fullerton, California, since 1971. Chuck's radio program, "Insight for Living," began in 1979. In addition to his church and radio ministries, Chuck enjoys writing. He has authored numerous books and booklets on a variety of subjects.

Based on the outlines and transcripts of Chuck's sermons, the study guide text is co-authored by Ken Gire, a graduate of Texas Christian University and Dallas Theological Seminary. He also wrote the Living Insights sections.

Editor in Chief:
Cynthia Swindoll

Coauthor of Text:
Ken Gire

Assistant Editor:
Glenda Schlahta

Copyediting Supervisor:
Marty Anderson

Copy Editor:
Connie Laser

Art Director:
Steven Mitchell

Designer:
Diana Vasquez

Production Artists:
Gary Lett and Diana Vasquez

Typographer:
Bob Haskins

Director, Communications Division:
Carla Beck

Project Manager:
Alene Cooper

Print Production Manager:
Deedee Snyder

Assistant Production Manager:
John Norton

Printer:
Frye and Smith

Notice

ISBN 0-8499-8416-5

Printed in the United States of America.

COVER DRAWING: Original print of Gustave Doré's *Esther Confounding Haman*, from The Bettmann Archive. Hand tinted by Diana Vasquez.

CONTENTS

INTRODUCTION

I have a confession to make. Not until I undertook this verse-by-verse exposition of Esther had I ever made a serious study of her life. I knew who she was, and I understood, in a general manner, the plot of her story; but little did I realize how beautifully it fit into our own times.

Now that the work is complete, I cannot describe the depth of my gratitude for this rather obscure and often-overlooked book in the Old Testament. As you work your way through these chapters, you will be amazed at the relevance of the message. Though God's name does not once appear in the book, His hand is on every life and His will is in every decision. You will love the way He sovereignly weaves the threads of His purpose into the events that transpire.

So . . . welcome to another opportunity to discover truth to live by, from an ancient scroll most people have never even read. It won't be long before you will be enchanted by Esther's captivating charm and challenged by her unswerving courage.

Chuck Swindoll

PUTTING TRUTH
INTO ACTION

K nowledge apart from application falls short of God's desire for
His children. He wants us to apply what we learn so that we
will change and grow. This study guide was prepared with these
goals in mind. As you go through the following pages, we hope
your desire to discover biblical truth will grow as your understanding
of God's Word increases, and that you will be encouraged to apply
what you've learned.

To assist you in your study, we've included a section called
Living Insights at the end of each lesson. These exercises will
challenge you to study further and to think of specific ways
to put your discoveries into action.

There are many ways to use this guide—in personal devotions,
group studies, discussions with friends and family, and Sunday school
classes. And, of course, it's an ideal study aid when you're listening
to its corresponding "Insight for Living" radio series.

To benefit most from this study guide, we would encourage you
to consider it a spiritual journal. That's why we've included space
in the Living Insights for recording your thoughts and discoveries.
We hope you'll return to those sections often for review and encouragement as you continue to grow in your walk with Christ.

Ken Gire

Ken Gire
Coauthor of Text
Author of Living Insights

ESTHER

A Woman for Such a Time as This

Chapter 1

GOD'S INVISIBLE PROVIDENCE

Survey of Esther

Although Shakespeare never appears in his plays, his presence is pervasive. Every act, every scene, every line of dialogue bears the imprint of his pen. He is the genius behind all the characters, each twist of plot, every poignant ending.

As far as the dramas in Scripture are concerned, the Book of Esther is an anomaly. It is the only book in the Bible that doesn't mention God's name. But like Shakespeare's plays, every page bears testimony to its author. Behind each scene you can see the shadow of the Almighty directing from the wings.

More than any other biblical book, Esther is a tribute to the invisible providence of God. Although we never actually hear or see God in the story, we have an overwhelming sense of confidence that He is just offstage, cueing the characters and orchestrating the drama to preserve His people from a tragic ending.

The Book of Esther is often like the dramas played out in our everyday lives. For seldom when enemies are on our heels are our Red Seas parted. Seldom when disaster is at our door are we warned by angelic visitors. Seldom when we are in need of direction are we instructed by God from a burning bush. And neither was Esther.

It's easy to see God in the miraculous. It's not so easy to see Him in the mundane. But that's where most of us live. We live without seeing handwriting on the wall or hearing thunder from Sinai. We live with God not centerstage but directing unobtrusively from the wings.

This is all the more reason why we need to be sensitive to His voice—so we can be aware of and attentive to the subtle ways in which He works. And no book will sharpen our spiritual senses more than Esther.

Gaining a Deeper Understanding of God

Before we plumb the depths of the Book of Esther, we want to take a few soundings on the unfathomable subject of God. It's easy to put God in a box or relegate Him to an outline or a table of contents. But God refuses tidy summary. He refuses to be confined by our conventional wisdom. It's important to understand how mysterious God is if we are ever to make sense of the mysterious ways in which He works.

The Mind of God—His Unsearchable Judgments

Our searching the mind of God is a little like a minnow surveying the ocean. At best, we'll only see what lies in front of our tiny eyes, but we'll miss the depth and the breadth of its watery secrets. As Isaiah the prophet wrote:

"For My thoughts are not your thoughts,
Neither are your ways My ways," declares the Lord.
"For as the heavens are higher than the earth,
So are My ways higher than your ways,
And My thoughts than your thoughts." (Isa. 55:8–9)

The Will of God—His Unfathomable Ways

Like the cold, dark depths of the ocean, the ways of God are often cloaked in mystery.

Oh, the depth of the riches both of the wisdom and knowledge of God! How unsearchable are His judgments and unfathomable His ways! For who has known the mind of the Lord, or who became His counselor? (Rom. 11:33–34)

The Power of God—His Sovereign Control

The power of God is beautifully described in a doxology in Daniel 4:34b–35.

"For His dominion is an everlasting dominion,
And His kingdom endures from generation to generation.
And all the inhabitants of the earth are accounted as nothing,

But He does according to His will in the host of
heaven
And among the inhabitants of earth;
And no one can ward off His hand
Or say to Him, 'What hast Thou done?' "

These gilded words come on the heels of a humiliating journey
that took King Nebuchadnezzar from insanity to recovery. Once
meretriciously robed in his own arrogance, the king was stripped of
his sanity and made to see who really ruled the throne of heaven.
Having been crushed under the mighty hand of God, the king
finally acknowledged the pervasiveness of God's power.

The Presence of God—His Invisible Providence

The word *providence* is derived from the Latin word *provideo.*
The prefix *pro* means "before"; the root *video* means "I see." As
monarch over heaven and earth, God sees events before they happen. He can see the future with precise clarity because He is the
one who works events according to His perfect plan. Even while
things appear to be out of hand or off course, God is there, working
invisibly behind the scenes (see Eccles. 7:13–14).

Even though the seasons change dramatically, even though na-
tions rise and fall on the world landscape, and even though econo-
mies tower to prosperity or topple to ruin, God never changes. From
everlasting to everlasting, He is God and His kingdom remains
unshakable (Ps. 46, 90:1–2; Isa. 40:6–8).

Make no mistake about it. God will have His way. Though He
remains invisible, He is in no way indifferent.

Seeing the Invisible Workings of God

Before the curtain rises on the drama of Esther, and before the
houselights dim, let's take a look at the playbill introducing us to
the cast.

The Characters in the Book

The first is a king named Ahasuerus.

> Now it took place in the days of Ahasuerus, the
> Ahasuerus who reigned from India to Ethiopia over
> 127 provinces, in those days as King Ahasuerus sat
> on his royal throne which was in Susa the capital.
> (Esther 1:1–2)

This king is also known in Scripture as Xerxes. He was a Persian king whose fame extended from India to Ethiopia. Under his reign were thousands of Jews who had chosen not to return to Palestine under the direction of Zerubbabel, Ezra, or Nehemiah. The word *Jews* is mentioned over fifty times in Esther, showing that the spotlight is turned on these members of the cast.

The second character in the cast is a queen named Vashti. She was a strong-willed, independent-minded woman who refused to cooperate with her husband's drunken demands. We first meet her in 1:9.

> Queen Vashti also gave a banquet for the women in the palace which belonged to King Ahasuerus.

The third character to make his stage entrance is a man named Haman. He is the antagonist, a wicked, anti-Semitic officer in the king's court. He is a man of conceit, wealth, influence, and deception. We see him profiled in chapter 3.

> After these events King Ahasuerus promoted Haman, the son of Hammedatha the Agagite, and advanced him and established his authority over all the princes who were with him. And all the king's servants who were at the king's gate bowed down and paid homage to Haman; for so the king had commanded concerning him. But Mordecai neither bowed down nor paid homage. . . . Then the king took his signet ring from his hand and gave it to Haman, the son of Hammedatha the Agagite, the enemy of the Jews. (vv. 1–2, 10)

The protagonist upon which the plot turns is a godly Jew named Mordecai. We are first introduced to him in 2:5–6.

> Now there was a Jew in Susa the capital whose name was Mordecai, the son of Jair, the son of Shimei, the son of Kish, a Benjamite, who had been taken into exile from Jerusalem with the captives who had been exiled with Jeconiah king of Judah, whom Nebuchadnezzar the king of Babylon had exiled.

We read in the very next verse that Mordecai raised the orphan Esther, who later turns out to be the heroine of the story.

And he was bringing up Hadassah, that is Esther, his uncle's daughter, for she had neither father nor mother. Now the young lady was beautiful of form and face, and when her father and her mother died, Mordecai took her as his own daughter. (v. 7)

She was a lowly Jewish woman who was as dazzling in outer beauty as she was in inner beauty. In fact, her name is the Persian name for "star," and she later ascended to the throne as queen after Vashti had a meteoric fall from the king's grace.

The Plot of the Book

The plot of Esther revolves around the survival of the Jews, who stood precariously on the threshold of a holocaust. Mordecai's refusal to pay Haman homage enraged the petty leader so much that he determined to make the whole Jewish population pay with their lives (3:2b–6, 8–13).

Word of their impending doom spread throughout the Jewish community (4:1–3). Realizing that the fate of his people hung by the thread of Esther's relationship to the king, Mordecai appeals to the queen.

He asks her to do a courageous thing—to stand alone before the king (vv. 13–17). Rising to the occasion of her need, God grants Esther the wisdom to devise a strategy that will eliminate the archenemy of her people. She invites both Haman and the king to a banquet where the king has vowed to hear what is troubling the queen and grant her wish (5:6–8).

Meanwhile, Haman is elated at the invitation. But as he passes the defiant Mordecai, who again refuses to pay him homage, his elation turns to infuriation. And at the advice of his wife, Haman erects a gallows from which he plans to hang Mordecai (vv. 12–14).

Then God providentially uses insomnia to awaken in the king an awareness of Mordecai's past heroism—heroism that had once saved the king's life. He decides that Mordecai should be exalted (6:1–10). So instead of putting a noose around Mordecai's neck, Haman is ordered to drape a robe of honor over his shoulders. Haman comes to the royal banquet, stewing over the sudden reversal of Mordecai's fate. Little does he realize the hot water he is about to be in. At the table, Esther reveals the plot against her people. The king asks the perpetrator's identity and Esther points her finger at Haman. In a sudden rage, the king sentences the archvillain to be hanged. And hanged he is—on the very gallows he had erected for Mordecai (7:10).

The Message of the Book of Esther

Though God is invisible, He is invincible. That is the message of the Book of Esther. The invisible God who may appear to be absent is the invincible God who is working out His best plan.

That is not only true for a young woman and her people in ancient Persia; that's true for us today in the twentieth century.

Go back to Esther 7:10 and let your mind linger over the incredible reversal of fates—those of Haman and Mordecai.

The gallows stood like a seven-and-a-half-story skeleton, gaunt and waiting. Haman was strategically positioned in the government to grease the gears of the political machine to obliterate the Jewish people. Unknown to the king's court, Mordecai was first on the list of political dissidents to be disposed of. Yet through Esther, a beautiful but inexperienced ingenue, God's invincible providence turned everything around.

Responding to the Quiet Promptings of God

Esther realized that God had raised her to a position of prominence for a reason. But to understand that reason, she had to ignore her palatial surroundings and listen to the still, small voice of providence. Psalm 46 commands us to do the same. It is a terse command of only eight words, yet those eight simple words are revolutionary: "Be still, and know that I am God" (v. 10a KJV). The New American Standard Bible translates it, "Cease striving and know that I am God." The Living Bible says, "Stand silent! . . ." The Hebrew literally means, "Let go, relax."

What will happen when we do? We'll learn what Esther learned —that God, though invisible, is invincible. But we will only learn that if we listen.

> Whoever will listen will hear the speaking Heaven. This is definitely not the hour when men take kindly to an exhortation to *listen,* for listening is not today a part of popular religion. We are at the opposite end of the pole from there. Religion has accepted the monstrous heresy that noise, size, activity and bluster make a man dear to God. But we may

take heart. To a people caught in the tempest of the last great conflict God says, "Be still, and know that I am God," and still He says it, as if He means to tell us that our strength and safety lie not in noise but in silence.[1]

Certainly that was true for the strength and safety of the Jewish nation under Ahasuerus. And certainly that is true for us as well.

—Following the Living Insights section, you will find a chart that provides a helpful overview of the Book of Esther.

 ## Living Insights

In the eighteenth century, William Cowper wrote this hymn:

God moves in a mysterious way,
His wonders to perform;
He plants His footsteps in the sea,
And rides upon the storm.

Deep in unfathomable mines
Of neverfailing skill,
He treasures up His bright designs,
And works His sov'reign will. . . .

Judge not the Lord by feeble sense,
But trust Him for His grace;
Behind a frowning providence
He hides a smiling face.[2]

Another Bible character who experienced God's providence, as Esther did, was Joseph. Plot the mysterious way in which God moved in this man's life.

Genesis 37 _____

_____

1. A. W. Tozer, *The Pursuit of God* (Wheaton, Ill.: Tyndale House Publishers, n.d.), p. 80.

2. William Cowper, "God Moves in a Mysterious Way," in *Hymns of Worship and Remembrance* (Topeka, Kans.: Gospel Perpetuating Fund Publishers, 1960), no. 311.

Genesis 39 _____

_____

Genesis 40 _____

_____

Genesis 41 _____

_____

Genesis 42 _____

_____

Genesis 45:1–8 _____

_____

It's easy for us to look back on Joseph's life and see behind a frowning providence God's smiling face. But it probably wasn't so easy for Joseph when he was sold into slavery by his jealous brothers.

How might God's ultimate purpose for Joseph have been thwarted if Joseph had become embittered toward his brothers?

_____

_____

_____

_____

How might God's ultimate purpose for you be thwarted by bitterness?

_____

_____

_____

_____

For some biblical counsel on bitterness, see Ephesians 4:31–32 and Hebrews 12:15.

Living Insights

In Psalm 46, the world is being dashed apart by earthquakes and tidal waves. Yet in the midst of that calamitous uncertainty, the psalmist discovers one thing he can count on—God. He can cease his striving because "The Lord of hosts is with us; The God of Jacob is our stronghold" (v. 11).

Perhaps the world you live in is falling apart around you, as well. You may be facing a life-threatening illness or major surgery. Your body may be twisted from debilitating pain. You may carry unbearable emotional stress home with you from work. If you're a student, you may be buried under the books. Maybe you suffer the sharp pain of a fractured relationship—one you've tried to restore, but it just won't mend. Maybe your career is uncertain or your job security precarious. Maybe there is a moral war you're struggling with and you're already feeling the incriminating introspection brought on by defeat.

Whatever mountains are crumbling around you, take the high ground and stop striving. *Initially, be quiet.* Listen to the whisper of God behind the roar of your circumstances. You can hear Him, even in the whirlwind, but you have to be still to listen. Then, *ultimately, be convinced.* Eventually God will change your circumstances, but in the meantime He wants to change you. Be assured that God is for you, not against you; that He is working behind the scenes for your highest good (Rom. 8:28–30).

In the following space, write down what you hear when you calm yourself to listen to the still, quiet voice of God beneath the roar of your circumstances.

_____

_____

_____

_____

_____

_____

_____

A Survey of Esther

Key verses: 4:14–16   **Key thought:** God at work behind the scenes.   **Key word:** *Jew* (51 times)

Uniqueness: The name of God is never once mentioned, nor is Esther quoted by one New Testament writer.

God's Providence among His People . . .						
During Hard Times				During Happy Times		
King's Banquet	Haman's Edict	Queen's Obedience . . .	God's Deliverance	Mordecai's Edict	Jews' Rejoicing (8:15–17)	*Shalom!*
Honoring the Kingdom		to Her God	Mordecai Honored		Enemies Destroyed	
Honoring the Queen		to Herself	Haman Hanged		Feast Established	
CHAPTERS 1–2	CHAPTER 3	CHAPTERS 4–5	CHAPTERS 6–7	CHAPTER 8	CHAPTER 9	CHAPTER 10
THREAT AND TRUST				DELIVERANCE AND PRAISE		
Feast of the King / Feast of the Queen				Feast of the Nation		
483 B.C.			→			473 B.C.

Chapter 2

"THERE SHE GOES...
MISS PERSIA!"

Esther 1:1–2:7

Winston Churchill had an appointment with Destiny. But he was oblivious to the calendar Destiny kept—that is, until May 10, 1939, when he discovered his name inked in its appointment book.

The morning of May 10 dawned in London with news of a German offensive. Holland and Belgium had been invaded, and France was soon to be trodden under by the rapidly advancing Nazi boot.

At six o'clock that morning a message summoned Churchill to the royal palace. There the king asked him to mobilize the government against Hitler. By the end of the day Churchill had accepted a position he would hold for the duration of the war, one that would secure him a place of honor in history.

His journal records his feelings of that fateful night.

> During these last crowded days of the political crisis, my pulse had not quickened at any moment. I took it all as it came. But I cannot conceal from the reader of this truthful account that as I went to bed at about 3 A.M. I was conscious of a profound sense of relief. At last I had the authority to give directions over the whole scene. I felt as if I were walking with Destiny, and that all my past life had been but a preparation for this hour and for this trial.[1]

Certainly Esther must have felt similarly when she heard the fateful words of Mordecai:

> "For if you remain silent at this time, relief and deliverance will arise for the Jews from another place and you and your father's house will perish. And who knows whether you have not attained royalty for such a time as this?" (Esther 4:14)

---

1. Winston Churchill, quoted in *Turning Point*, ed. Philip Dunaway and George de Kay (New York, N.Y.: Random House, 1958), p. 284.

"For such a time as this"—Esther's appointment with Destiny. Like Churchill, her whole life had been "but a preparation for this hour and for this trial." And now was the time for her to step forward and keep that appointment.

Uneventful Beginnings—Unbelievable Endings

Esther went from the humdrum life of an orphan to the palatial life as queen to one of the most powerful men in the world. From there she went on to become a heroine and secured a place of honor in Israel's history. Unbelievable, isn't it?

The New Testament records a number of incidents that started uneventfully yet ended unbelievably. The birth of our Lord is one. The night was like any night. There were no handbills passed announcing the birth. There was no reception by the city fathers. Yet on that silent night in Bethlehem, God entered the world. And since then, the ripples of that event have touched every shore on the face of the earth.

Another incident was the day of Christ's resurrection. Just another sleepy Sunday morning for the majority of people in Jerusalem. And yet that chilly pastel morning gave a dawn of hope to a world shrouded in the dark finality of the grave.

The day of Christ's return will be another day that starts out routinely. Alarm clocks will go off as usual. People will bustle off on their normal schedules—to work, to school, to appointments. But suddenly, curtains of clouds will part and the Lord Himself will descend dramatically.

The Old Testament has some equally compelling examples. The day the great Flood swallowed every civilization on earth. The day Moses encountered the burning bush and was commissioned to lead the Exodus. The day a simple young shepherd boy was anointed by Samuel to become the greatest king Israel had ever known.

Esther's Uneventful Beginning

God is still in the business of bringing about unbelievable endings from uneventful beginnings. What seems mundane to you now may simply be the preparation for something monumental. The way it was for Esther.

Little did this insignificant orphan girl know the incredible way God would work in her life. When she crawled out of bed that day with mussed hair and morning breath, little did she realize that she would be entering a beauty pageant whose prize would be to share the throne of the Medo-Persian Empire.

The Book of Esther begins blandly enough: "Now it took place in the days of Ahasuerus. . . ." The Hebrew is just as lackluster: "And it was. . . ." The NIV captures the ordinariness of the beginning with the words, "This is what happened. . . ." But what follows is anything but dull.

A Casual Glimpse into a Persian Palace

Verses 1–2 set the stage for the resplendent opening scene.

> Now it took place in the days of Ahasuerus, the Ahasuerus who reigned from India to Ethiopia over 127 provinces, in those days as King Ahasuerus sat on his royal throne which was in Susa the capital.

What took place? A party . . . and *what* a party! The king decided to regale his kingdom with a banquet so elaborate it made the famed birthday bashes of the late Malcolm Forbes look like brown-bag luncheons on the back lawn.

> In the third year of his reign, he gave a banquet for all his princes and attendants, the army officers of Persia and Media, the nobles, and the princes of his provinces being in his presence. And he displayed the riches of his royal glory and the splendor of his great majesty for many days, 180 days. And when these days were completed, the king gave a banquet lasting seven days for all the people who were present in Susa the capital, from the greatest to the least, in the court of the garden of the king's palace. There were hangings of fine white and violet linen held by cords of fine purple linen on silver rings and marble columns, and couches of gold and silver on a mosaic pavement of porphyry, marble, mother-of-pearl, and precious stones. Drinks were served in golden vessels of various kinds, and the royal wine was plentiful according to the king's bounty. And the drinking was done according to the law, there was no compulsion, for so the king had given orders to each official of his household that he should do according to the desires of each person. (vv. 3–8)

Meanwhile, the king's wife threw a party of her own.

Queen Vashti also gave a banquet for the women in the palace which belonged to King Ahasuerus. (v. 9)

A Public Conflict between the King and Queen

After a week of festivities, the stag party Ahasuerus hosted for the men got out of hand.

On the seventh day, when the heart of the king was merry with wine, he commanded Mehuman, Biztha, Harbona, Bigtha, Abagtha, Zethar, and Carkas, the seven eunuchs who served in the presence of King Ahasuerus, to bring Queen Vashti before the king with her royal crown in order to display her beauty to the people and the princes, for she was beautiful. (vv. 10–11)

The word translated "crown" literally means "turban." Some Jewish scholars suggest that the command was for Vashti to come unveiled to show off her beautiful face. Others suggest that the command was for her to come wearing only the turban, thus showing off everything.

Whatever the royal order that came to her out of the banqueting-hall exactly was, the brave queen refused to obey it. Her beauty was her own and her husband's: it was not for open show among hundreds of half-drunk men.[2]

But Queen Vashti refused to come at the king's command delivered by the eunuchs. (v. 12a)

Queen Vashti represents a good example of the limits of a wife's submission. The command for a wife to submit to her husband is clear in Scripture (see Eph. 5:22–24). But it is not absolute and without limits. The woman does not give up her dignity as a human being when she becomes a wife. Neither should she allow her principles to be trodden underfoot by an unprincipled husband. Marriage does not give the husband license to pursue his basest sexual fantasies, and neither does it enslave the wife to fulfill them.

---

2. Alexander Whyte, *Bible Characters* (London, England: Oliphants, 1952), vol. 1, p. 419.

Nevertheless, the queen's refusal infuriated the king and spurred a heated debate about the effect her actions could have on the status quo.

> Then the king became very angry and his wrath burned within him. Then the king said to the wise men who understood the times—for it was the custom of the king so to speak before all who knew law and justice, and were close to him: Carshena, Shethar, Admatha, Tarshish, Meres, Marsena, and Memucan, the seven princes of Persia and Media who had access to the king's presence and sat in the first place in the kingdom—"According to law, what is to be done with Queen Vashti, because she did not obey the command of King Ahasuerus delivered by the eunuchs?" And in the presence of the king and the princes, Memucan said, "Queen Vashti has wronged not only the king but also all the princes, and all the peoples who are in all the provinces of King Ahasuerus. For the queen's conduct will become known to all the women causing them to look with contempt on their husbands by saying, 'King Ahasuerus commanded Queen Vashti to be brought in to his presence, but she did not come.' And this day the ladies of Persia and Media who have heard of the queen's conduct will speak in the same way to all the king's princes, and there will be plenty of contempt and anger." (Esther 1:12b–18)

Immediate Proclamation for All to Obey

In those days the king was supreme. His edicts were absolute, not legislation for congressional debate. This particular edict had two parts: the first regarded the queen (v. 19); the second regarded all marriages in the Medo-Persian Empire (vv. 20–22).

> "If it pleases the king, let a royal edict be issued by him and let it be written in the laws of Persia and Media so that it cannot be repealed, that Vashti should come no more into the presence of King Ahasuerus, and let the king give her royal position to another who is more worthy than she. And when the king's edict which he shall make is heard throughout all

his kingdom, great as it is, then all women will give honor to their husbands, great and small." And this word pleased the king and the princes, and the king did as Memucan proposed. So he sent letters to all the king's provinces, to each province according to its script and to every people according to their language, that every man should be the master in his own house and the one who speaks in the language of his own people. (vv. 19–22)

The salient point of the edict, as far as God's providence was concerned, is the clause, "let the king give her royal position to another." That clause prepared the way for Esther. And it illustrates the truth of Proverbs 21:1.

> The king's heart is like channels of water in the
> hand of the Lord;
> He turns it wherever He wishes.

The gears of providence may grind slowly, but they track perfectly the sovereign course the Lord has designed for them. And nobody—not even a powerful king—can stand in their way.

A Lingering Loneliness and a Creative Idea

Esther 2 begins in a nostalgic, almost melancholy, tone.

> After these things when the anger of King Ahasuerus had subsided, he remembered Vashti and what she had done and what had been decreed against her. (v. 1)

"After these things" is vague and does not precisely nail down the time. However, it was probably shortly after Ahasuerus had suffered defeat from the wars he waged on Greece in 480–479 B.C., taking into consideration the times mentioned in 2:12 and 16. This lapse of time would give the king's anger toward Vashti a chance to subside, leaving him lonely and nostalgic. It had been awhile since Ahasuerus had enjoyed the companionship of a queen, and he was despondent. His attendants took note of the lingering loneliness and prescribed a remedy.

> Then the king's attendants, who served him, said, "Let beautiful young virgins be sought for the king. And let the king appoint overseers in all the provinces

of his kingdom that they may gather every beautiful young virgin to Susa the capital, to the harem, into the custody of Hegai, the king's eunuch, who was in charge of the women; and let their cosmetics[3] be given them. Then let the young lady who pleases the king be queen in place of Vashti." And the matter pleased the king, and he did accordingly. (vv. 2–4)

An Unknown Man—An Obscure Woman

It almost seems something to raise eyebrows over, but God worked through a beauty pageant to providentially cross Esther's path with Ahasuerus'.

Now there was a Jew in Susa the capital whose name was Mordecai, the son of Jair, the son of Shimei, the son of Kish, a Benjamite, who had been taken into exile from Jerusalem with the captives who had been exiled with Jeconiah king of Judah, whom Nebuchadnezzar the king of Babylon had exiled. And he was bringing up Hadassah, that is Esther, his uncle's daughter, for she had neither father nor mother. Now the young lady was beautiful of form and face, and when her father and her mother died, Mordecai took her as his own daughter. (vv. 5–7)

See how this contestant's résumé read? She was a Jew and an orphan, raised by her cousin. Not much else is recorded about her—except that she was shapely and stunning. Yet she became the queen who would save the Jews from complete annihilation.

How God Still Works in Uneventful Times

Esther's life is a classic example of an uneventful beginning that led to an unbelievable ending. But that was ancient history. What about today? Does God still work through uneventful beginnings?

You bet He does. And here are three thoughts to keep in mind when you're muddling through a mundane Monday morning.

3. The Hebrew root "to rub, to polish, signifies purification and adornment with all kind of precious ointments." C. F. Keil, "I and II Kings, I and II Chronicles, Ezra, Nehemiah, Esther," *Commentary on the Old Testament in Ten Volumes*, by C. F. Keil and F. Delitzsch (Grand Rapids, Mich.: William B. Eerdmans Publishing Co., n.d.), vol. 3, p. 334. See also Esther 2:12.

God's plans are not hindered when events are secular or carnal. His power penetrates through the broken glass of a drunken banquet as well as through the stained glass of a Gothic cathedral.

God's purposes are not frustrated by moral or marital conflicts. The king, in all his drunken debauchery and cruel chauvinism, could not thwart the purposes of God. In reality, he was not king at all, but only one more pawn in the hand of God. And God could move him anywhere on the chessboard that He wanted (Prov. 21:1).

God's people are not excluded from high places because of handicap or hardship. Esther was a foreigner and an orphan. By all human odds it was a million-to-one chance that she would even be invited to the pageant, let alone win it. But by God's providence, it happened.

Hebrews 11:1 says, "Faith is the assurance of things hoped for, the conviction of things not seen." Throughout the marbled halls of that chapter are statues of ordinary men and women who believed God in extraordinary ways. Many lived much of their lives as Esther did, in uneventful times. Yet from the nomadic existence of Abraham dwelling in tents to the staid existence of David tending sheep, God providentially worked to script unbelievable endings to the stories of their lives.

Want to hear something even more incredible? God wants to do the same with your life.

 ## Living Insights

God still works in uneventful times to providentially produce unbelievable endings. Let's review the three application points from our study to see how they apply to our own lives.

God's plans are not hindered when events are secular or carnal. He can work in the Oval Office as well as the pastor's study. Charles Colson, special counsel to former President Nixon and convicted Watergate conspirator, is evidence of that. In his book *Born Again,* he recounts how God reached through the curtains of the White House and through the bars in a prison cell to pull him into the kingdom and put him into the ministry.

Is there some secular circumstance, maybe even a sinful circumstance, touching your life right now? Maybe your job environment is intolerable. Maybe a neighbor is antagonistic toward you. Maybe a friend has wandered far from the faith.

Write down a circumstance that you feel is virtually hopeless.

_____

_____

_____

Now covenant with God to pray for His providential interven-tion through everyday events to produce an unbelievable ending. *God's purposes are not frustrated by moral or marital conflicts.* God can construct His purposes from the rubble of a failed life. He can make mortar from the mud of an affair. He can design beautiful stained glass windows from the broken fragments of our lives.

What is the moral or marital conflict that is presently frustrating you?

_____

_____

_____

What kind of unbelievable ending would you script for that circum-stance if you could be God for a day?

_____

_____

_____

How much of your prayer time is devoted to asking for that ending?

_____

God's people are not excluded from high places because of handicap or hardship. Is there a handicap or hardship that you feel is hindering you from advancement? Maybe it's a lack of financial resources. Maybe it's a fear of people. Maybe it's a wheelchair or old age or your weight. Whatever it is, God can overcome that obstacle.

Write the following verse on a notecard and put it someplace where you will see it every day to strengthen you in discouraging times.

> "'For I know the plans that I have for you,' declares
> the Lord, 'plans for welfare and not for calamity to
> give you a future and a hope.'" (Jer. 29:11)

Living Insights

A character in this story who is often overshadowed by Esther is Queen Vashti. Whatever else may be said about her, she was a woman of conviction. She stood up to the most powerful man in the land at the cost of her marriage and her throne.

Not many people would be able to stand so firm in their convictions. How about you? Does any principle mean so much to you that you would be willing to risk losing your job over it? Is there any principle you would be willing to risk a significant relationship for?

_____

_____

Most of us tend to live by expedience rather than by principle, making decisions not on the basis of our convictions but on the basis of possible consequences. Dietrich Bonhoeffer once said: "If we claim to be Christians, there is no room for expediency."[4]

Describe a time when you compromised your convictions because of the consequences that might result.

_____

_____

_____

_____

Looking back, how do you feel about that incident?

_____

_____

Joseph is an inspiring Old Testament example of someone who lived by his convictions rather than by anticipated consequences (see Gen. 39). Turning to the New Testament, we find another stirring example in Stephen (Acts 6:8–7:60). If you are fearing the consequences of standing up for your convictions, read Matthew 10:16–33 and Romans 8:31–39 for encouragement.

4. Quoted by G. Leibholz in "Memoir," in Dietrich Bonhoeffer's _The Cost of Discipleship_, rev. ed. (1949; reprint, New York, N.Y.: Macmillan Co., 1963), p. 25.

Chapter 3
QUEENLIKE QUALITIES OF A LOVELY LADY
Esther 2:8–20

In many ways, there is not a more powerful creature on earth than a woman. One man has noted:

> Women have more strength in their looks, than we have in our laws; and more power by their tears, than we have by our arguments.[1]

Another has marveled:

> Women are the poetry of the world in the same sense as the stars are the poetry of heaven. —Clear, light-giving, harmonious, they are the terrestrial planets that rule the destinies of mankind.[2]

There is truth in the age-old maxim "the hand that rocks the cradle rules the world." That hand is the strong yet tender one of the mother, who not only bears the children but rears them as well. It is no wonder that when the cameras are turned on the 250-pound football player who's just scored a touchdown or recovered a fumble, the first words to come out of his mouth are "Hi, Mom!"

But as if raising a houseful of children isn't enough of a job, the married woman has at least one other demanding career—that of a wife. She is there for a husband either as the wind beneath his wings or the one who lets the air out of his tires. Proverbs talks about both kinds of wives. The one to be admired is the excellent wife of Proverbs 31. Her worth is far above jewels. She is valuable to her husband because most men's decisions would lack depth and perspective without her. As Victor Hugo, the famous French novelist, wrote: "Men have sight; women insight."[3]

---

1. J. F. Saville, quoted in *The New Dictionary of Thoughts*, comp. Tryon Edwards, rev. and enl. by C. N. Catrevas, Jonathan Edwards, and Ralph Emerson Browns (Standard Book Co., 1966), p. 733.

2. Francis Hargrave, in *The New Dictionary of Thoughts*, p. 735.

3. In *The New Dictionary of Thoughts*, p. 738.

God-given Strengths Found in Women

Any list of a woman's strengths would come up short, but we would like to attempt that list anyway by mentioning four strengths, more often held by women than men, that particularly stand out.

1. *Intuition:* that sixth sense which enables her to see through situations, to sense the unspoken, and to perceive what most men fail to see.
2. *Endurance:* that incredible ability to handle pain, to stay at a task through insuperable odds, and to persevere.
3. *Responsiveness:* that willingness to demonstrate her feelings, to react, to show warmth and affection.
4. *Vulnerability:* that courage to express weakness, to admit fear, and to ask for help.

The book of Proverbs describes several other traits that are true of the godly woman.

A gracious woman attains honor. (11:16a)

An excellent wife is the crown of her husband. (12:4a)

He who finds a wife finds a good thing,
And obtains favor from the Lord. (18:22)

House and wealth are an inheritance from fathers,
But a prudent wife is from the Lord. (19:14)

But the most polished description of the ideal woman is found in Proverbs 31:10–31. It was written by the mother of a king and is placed in a climactic position at the conclusion of the book. We'll take a good look at this incredible woman a little later in our Living Insights. But for now, let your mind skim through the pages of the past to glimpse some of the heroines of yesteryear.

History is full of remarkable women—Joan of Arc, Florence Nightingale, Madame Curie—courageous women, full of fight and fortitude, vision and virtue, grace and truth. Within the pages of biblical history, too, are chapters of feminine courage and character —Jochebed, the mother of Moses; Hannah, the mother of Samuel; Rahab, who hid the spies; Deborah, who led Israel; Mary, the mother of our Lord. And then there's the heroine of our story, Esther.

Esther: The King's Favorite . . . and Why

Two books in the Bible bear the names of women—Ruth and Esther. And though the account of Esther is only a few pages long, her life speaks volumes to us today.

Let's pick up the story in the powder room of the palace, where the contestants are putting on their makeup for the Miss Persia pageant.

> So it came about when the command and decree of the king were heard and many young ladies were gathered to Susa the capital into the custody of Hegai, that Esther was taken to the king's palace into the custody of Hegai, who was in charge of the women. (Esther 2:8)

The verb *was taken* doesn't connote volunteerism. In fact, this verb can mean "taken by force." Some Jewish scholars accept this interpretation, although there is nothing in the text to reinforce that idea; however, it could well be that Esther was reluctant to participate. After all, she was a Jew, and marrying a Gentile was against the code of conduct handed down from early Jewish law.

When you imagine how competitive the contestants must have been at the prospect of being chosen queen, Esther's reluctance comes across as a wonderfully attractive quality. Undoubtedly, Esther's inner beauty eclipsed the jealous, greedy, self-absorbed women of the harem, and that's what caught Hegai's eye. In the passages that follow, at least six attractive qualities stand out.

The first one is *a grace-filled charm and elegance*.

> Now the young lady pleased him and found favor with him. So he quickly provided her with her cosmetics and food, gave her seven choice maids from the king's palace, and transferred her and her maids to the best place in the harem. (v. 9)

In Hebrew, the first sentence in verse 9 literally states: "She lifted up grace before his face." This quality exudes a pleasantness in the presence of others. So fragrant was this quality that its aroma prompted Hegai to act "quickly" and to treat her preferentially.

The second quality is *an unusual restraint and control*.

> Esther did not make known her people or her kindred. (v. 10a)

Esther knew the value of verbal restraint. Even when she became queen, she kept the secret Mordecai had told her to keep (v. 20). That not only created an air of mystery about her, but an aura of charm as well.

The third characteristic is *a continually teachable spirit.*

> For Mordecai had instructed her that she should not make them known. (v. 10b)

Becoming a finalist in the pageant didn't go to Esther's head. Neither did becoming queen (v. 20). Isn't it lovely to come across a woman of such stunning beauty who also has such a student's spirit, such a willingness to listen and learn? Sometimes, the more gifted we are—or the more physically endowed, the more popular, the more prominent in position—the less teachable we become. Which is unfortunate, because none of those gifts gives us a corner on wisdom.

The fourth quality is *an unselfish modesty and authenticity.*

> Now when the turn of each young lady came to go in to King Ahasuerus, after the end of her twelve months under the regulations for the women—for the days of their beautification were completed as follows: six months with oil of myrrh and six months with spices and the cosmetics for women—the young lady would go in to the king in this way: anything that she desired was given her to take with her from the harem to the king's palace. In the evening she would go in and in the morning she would return to the second harem, to the custody of Shaashgaz, the king's eunuch who was in charge of the concubines. She would not again go in to the king unless the king delighted in her and she was summoned by name. (vv. 12–14)

Clearly, the process of preparing for the pageant was lengthy and expensive. Imagine the setting. It must have been like going into Bloomingdales or Neiman-Marcus and being able to take any of the dresses off the rack, any of the jewelry from the showcases, and a whole line of cosmetic products—all at no cost. No doubt, most of the women went on an extravagant and unrestrained shopping spree. Except for Esther.

Now when the turn of Esther, the daughter of Abihail
the uncle of Mordecai who had taken her as his
daughter, came to go in to the king, she did not
request anything except what Hegai, the king's eunuch who was in charge of the women, advised.
And Esther found favor in the eyes of all who saw
her. (v. 15)

The fifth quality is *a winsomeness, regardless of her surroundings.*
Did you note in verse 15 that Esther made no extravagant demands? She listened attentively to Hegai and complied with his
advice. Her winsomeness and charm not only compelled Hegai but
totally captivated the king. Compared to the other women in the
harem, she stood out in Ahasuerus' eyes like a stately swan in a
duck pond.

So Esther was taken to King Ahasuerus to his
royal palace in the tenth month which is the month
Tebeth, in the seventh year of his reign. And the
king loved Esther more than all the women, and she
found favor and kindness with him more than all the
virgins, so that he set the royal crown on her head
and made her queen instead of Vashti. (vv. 16–17)

The sixth quality is *a humble respect for authority.*

Then the king gave a great banquet, Esther's banquet, for all his princes and his servants; he also
made a holiday for the provinces and gave gifts according to the king's bounty.
And when the virgins were gathered together
the second time, then Mordecai was sitting at the
king's gate. Esther had not yet made known her
kindred or her people, even as Mordecai had commanded her, for Esther did what Mordecai told her
as she had done when under his care. (vv. 18–20)

Now was Esther's golden opportunity to revel in her newly ac-
quired position of power—to throw off the shackels of accountabil-
ity. But she resisted the temptation. She still submitted to Mordecai's
advice, even though she was queen. And it is that respect for his
counsel that will later catapult her to the heights of heroism.

Practical Counsel for Modern-Day Esthers

The primary applications for this lesson seem to be aimed at women, but the principles run deeper than gender distinctions. They apply to men as well, for the cultivation of character—not cosmetics—is the focal point of our study. We're addressing what we are on the inside, not what we smear on the outside. So if you'll turn on the lights and squint in the mirror, we'll see what can be done for that hidden person of the heart.

First, ask God to cultivate within you a discontent for the superficial and, at the same time, a desire for the spiritual. Anne Morrow Lindbergh says it best in her excellent book *Gift from the Sea:*

> I am seeking perhaps what Socrates asked for in the prayer from the *Phaedrus* when he said, "May the outward and inward man be at one." I would like to achieve a state of inner spiritual grace from which I could function and give as I was meant to in the eye of God.[4]

Second, trust God to control the circumstances around you. Remember Esther. The atmosphere of such a competitive beauty pageant is a difficult context in which to preserve the beauty of the inner self. Yet in this soil Esther blossomed.

 ## Living Insights

In 1 Peter 3:3–4, the apostle exhorts women not to gild the outward picture frame but to concentrate on painting a masterpiece on the canvas of the inner person.

> And let not your adornment be merely external— braiding the hair, and wearing gold jewelry, or putting on dresses; but let it be the hidden person of the heart, with the imperishable quality of a gentle and quiet spirit, which is precious in the sight of God.

Does Peter suggest that it's wrong for a woman to fix her hair or wear jewelry?   Yes ☐   No ☐

---

4. Anne Morrow Lindbergh, *Gift from the Sea* (New York, N.Y.: Pantheon Books, 1955), pp. 23–24.

What word in verse 3 lets us know the answer? _____

What is the contrast between verses 3 and 4?

_____

_____

_____

_____

How would you define "a gentle and quiet spirit"?

_____

_____

_____

Read Isaiah 3:16–26, and describe God's reaction to our focusing too much on external appearances.

_____

_____

_____

What does our exclusive and intense focus on the physical reflect about ourselves? See Isaiah 3:16a.

_____

_____

_____

From 1 Samuel 16:7, what is God's focus?

_____

_____

_____

OK, ladies—it's time to scrub off the cosmetics and switch on the makeup mirror. But the mirror we want you to look into is not a physical one but a spiritual one—the mirror of God's Word (see James 1:22–25).

Turn to Proverbs 31 and take a good, hard look. Is it you in that mirror? Whether you are married or unmarried, put a check mark by the qualities you have in common with the excellent wife reflected in verses 10–31.

Verses

10 ☐	16 ☐	21 ☐	26 ☐
11 ☐	17 ☐	22 ☐	27 ☐
12 ☐	18 ☐	23 ☐	28 ☐
13 ☐	19 ☐	24 ☐	29 ☐
14 ☐	20 ☐	25 ☐	30 ☐
15 ☐			31 ☐

Of those you didn't check, which one stands out as the most glaring blemish on the face of that hidden person of the heart?

_____

What can you do to clear up that unsightly blemish?

_____

_____

_____

_____

_____

_____

_____

Chapter 4

AN EVIL INTERLUDE

Esther 2:21–3:15

If you were to look up the word *life* in heaven's thesaurus, one of the first synonyms you would find would be *pain.*

Life is filled with sharp corners and hard floors. Try as we may to cushion ourselves from the bumps and brace ourselves for the falls, pain is inescapable. It comes with the territory. We can't huddle ourselves away in some cave to avoid it. Neither can we hope that our faith will insulate us from the cold, hard realities of life. It certainly didn't with saints of old.

Innocent Job was covered with skin ulcers, faithful Daniel was thrown into a lion's den, godly Joseph was imprisoned. Courageous Paul was beaten, bold John the Baptist was beheaded, Spirit-filled Stephen was stoned . . . and even Jesus, the sinless Son of God, was tortured and crucified.

Speaking from his pain, Job tells us:

> "Man, who is born of woman,
> Is short-lived and full of turmoil." (Job 14:1)

The Living Bible distills his words into three succinct statements: "How frail is man, how few his days, how full of trouble!" Earlier in the book, Job remarks:

> "For man is born for trouble,
> As sparks fly upward." (5:7)

"Born for trouble." Isn't it time we stopped trying to escape the inescapable? Isn't it time we faced up to pain and suffering and hardship and affliction? Isn't it time we stopped skipping class and took our seats to learn the lessons pain has to teach?

Suffering: A Repeated Theme throughout Life

When we analyze life's troubles, the categories seem legion, don't they?

Categories of Suffering

There are disasters in the natural world: earthquakes, tornadoes, hurricanes, floods, mud slides, blizzards, droughts.

There are physical afflictions: injuries, birth defects, handicaps, disabilities, diseases, burns, assaults.

There are emotional traumas: phobias, depressions, neuroses, psychoses, self-image struggles.

There are domestic conflicts: husband-and-wife battles, parent-and-child problems, decisions about aging parents, arguments over finances.

Then there are national and international concerns: crime, drugs, gangs, war, economic worries on a global scale.

Job was right: "How frail is man, how few his days, how full of trouble!" (TLB).

Reaction to Suffering

In his book *The Road Less Traveled,* Scott Peck echoes what Job said thousands of years earlier.

> What makes life difficult is that the process of confronting and solving problems is a painful one. Problems, depending upon their nature, evoke in us frustration or grief or sadness or loneliness or guilt or regret or anger or fear or anxiety or anguish or despair. These are uncomfortable feelings, often very uncomfortable, often as painful as any kind of physical pain, sometimes equaling the very worst kind of physical pain. Indeed, it is *because* of the pain that events or conflicts engender in us that we call them problems. And since life poses an endless series of problems, life is always difficult and is full of pain as well as joy.[1]

Since pain is so pervasive, how should we react to it? First of all, we can never react correctly to life's pains and hurts unless we have the correct theological understanding of them. At the center of them all is Evil with a capital E. Evil entered the world when humanity morally stumbled and fell in the Garden of Eden (see Gen. 2:16–17, Rom. 5:12).

From that time a Pandora's box remained forever open. Pain, hardship, suffering, sorrow, and death flowed from Paradise Lost to pollute the entire earth (Gen. 3:16–19). No matter how pristine

1. M. Scott Peck, *The Road Less Traveled* (New York, N.Y.: Simon and Schuster, A Touchstone Book, 1978), p. 16.

the beauty of Eden had been, it now lay overgrown with thorns and thistles in a state of moral and physical ruin.

All this brings us back to our friend Esther, an unspoiled flower in the King of Persia's garden. But lurking in the shadows, casting its dark pallor over her queenly throne, is evil. With it, this evil brings pain and ultimately death.

Mutiny: A Minor Plot against the King

At this moment in our fairy tale story, we anticipate the idyllic ending, "and they lived happily ever after."

But the story takes a turn down a dark alley instead.

Secret Conspiracy

We pick up the story where two of the king's men are plotting from the shadowy recesses of their evil hearts.

> In those days, while Mordecai was sitting at the king's gate, Bigthan and Teresh, two of the king's officials from those who guarded the door, became angry and sought to lay hands on King Ahasuerus. But the plot became known to Mordecai, and he told Queen Esther, and Esther informed the king in Mordecai's name. (Esther 2:21–22)

Bigthan's and Teresh's anger toward the king festered into murder.

Swift Punishment

Word of the plot leaked out to Mordecai, and from him, through Esther to the king. The insurgents were sentenced to death, and before the ink was dry on the decree, they were history.

> Now when the plot was investigated and found to be so, they were both hanged on a gallows; and it was written in the Book of the Chronicles in the king's presence. (v. 23)

The tendency is to think that since evil was decisively dealt with, peace returned to the royal palace. Not so. It rears its ugly head again—this time, farther up the official ladder.

Vengeance: A Major Scheme against the Jews

Since Mordecai saved the king's life, you would think he would be first in line for a promotion to prime minister. But he is passed over—just another example that deserving people often get overlooked and that righteousness often goes unrewarded. It's unfair, but that's how life is.

The one who does get the promotion is Haman, an anti-Semite bent on Mordecai's destruction.

> After these events King Ahasuerus promoted Haman, the son of Hammedatha the Agagite, and advanced him and established his authority over all the princes who were with him. And all the king's servants who were at the king's gate bowed down and paid homage to Haman; for so the king had commanded concerning him. But Mordecai neither bowed down nor paid homage. Then the king's servants who were at the king's gate said to Mordecai, "Why are you transgressing the king's command?" Now it was when they had spoken daily to him and he would not listen to them, that they told Haman to see whether Mordecai's reason would stand; for he had told them that he was a Jew. When Haman saw that Mordecai neither bowed down nor paid homage to him, Haman was filled with rage. But he disdained to lay hands on Mordecai alone, for they had told him who the people of Mordecai were. (3:1–6a)

The roots of Haman's bitterness toward the Jews can be traced back to his family tree. He was a descendant of Agag, the Amalekite king whom Samuel finally killed. The Amalekites had remained bitter enemies of the Jews, and the feud was taken up by Haman. Prejudice is a vicious evil. And it's hereditary, passed down from generation to generation.

When Mordecai refused to bow down, the anti-Semitic hair on the back of Haman's neck stood on end. He became "filled with rage" (v. 5).

Mordecai refused to bow down for two reasons: (1) The act would be considered idolatry by a Jew, and (2) in no way did he want to show respect to an Amalekite, an avowed enemy of his people.

Plan for Extermination

Haman's hatred seethed in a caldron that spilled over not only on Mordecai but on all of Mordecai's people.

> Therefore Haman sought to destroy all the Jews, the
> people of Mordecai, who were throughout the whole
> kingdom of Ahasuerus. (v. 6b)

Haman is a prime example of just how deceitful and desperately wicked the human heart can be (see Jer. 17:9, Rom. 3:13–18). It was from the murky depths of hearts like Haman's that the Holocaust was dredged up. In the ominous shadows of the concentration camps, racial hatred laid in wait for Jewish blood, threatening the genocide of an entire race.

Haman had plenty of time to engineer the fate of the Jews as he waited for his number to come up to be brought before the king.

> In the first month, which is the month Nisan,
> in the twelfth year of King Ahasuerus, Pur, that is
> the lot, was cast before Haman from day to day and
> from month to month, until the twelfth month,
> that is the month Adar. Then Haman said to King
> Ahasuerus, "There is a certain people scattered and
> dispersed among the peoples in all the provinces of
> your kingdom; their laws are different from those of
> all other people, and they do not observe the king's
> laws, so it is not in the king's interest to let them
> remain." (Esther 3:7 8)

Haman then sweetens the rotten pot with a spice he hopes will appeal to the king's palate—a pinch of greed.

> "If it is pleasing to the king, let it be decreed that
> they be destroyed, and I will pay ten thousand talents of silver into the hands of those who carry on
> the king's business, to put into the king's treasuries."
> (v. 9)

Ten thousand talents of silver equaled 375 tons, estimated to represent two-thirds of the annual income of the entire Persian Empire. No doubt Haman planned to make good on his pledge by confiscating the assets of those he annihilated.

The plan sounds in the best interest of the empire, and the king gives it a "thumbs up."

> Then the king took his signet ring from his hand
> and gave it to Haman, the son of Hammedatha the

Agagite, the enemy of the Jews. And the king said to Haman, "The silver is yours, and the people also, to do with them as you please." (vv. 10–11)

Announcement to All

The entire plot had been synchronized like clockwork. The scribes were poised and ready to write. The ring on Haman's hand gave him the power of attorney to set the king's seal on any document he drafted. The couriers were ready to ride their steeds to all the provinces of the kingdom, and the heralds' lips were pursed to cry "Hear ye! Hear ye!" The gears were set in motion.

> Then the king's scribes were summoned on the thirteenth day of the first month, and it was written just as Haman commanded to the king's satraps, to the governors who were over each province, and to the princes of each people, each province according to its script, each people according to its language, being written in the name of King Ahasuerus and sealed with the king's signet ring. And letters were sent by couriers to all the king's provinces to destroy, to kill, and to annihilate all the Jews, both young and old, women and children, in one day, the thirteenth day of the twelfth month, which is the month Adar, and to seize their possessions as plunder. A copy of the edict to be issued as law in every province was published to all the peoples so that they should be ready for this day. The couriers went out impelled by the king's command while the decree was issued in Susa the capital; and while the king and Haman sat down to drink, the city of Susa was in confusion. (vv. 12–15)

The scene in the last verse is ironic—the king and Haman sitting down for a peaceful drink while the city stumbled over itself in bewilderment. Like Friday the thirteenth, this thirteenth of Adar loomed in the people's minds with a macabre foreboding. In just eleven months the streets would become tributaries of blood, rivers of racial hatred, red with anti-Semitism.

Thus falls the curtain on act 2 of our drama. And it doesn't look good for the Jewish people.

Wickedness: An Appropriate Response

Besides the two who were hanged, three male actors have performed in our drama so far: Mordecai, Haman, and King Ahasuerus. Each of these characters has something specific to teach us.

From Mordecai we learn this: *Always remember that someone will resent your independent devotion to the Lord.* Mordecai's loyalty to God prevented him from bowing his knee to Haman the prime minister. Our devotion to God should also keep us from compromising our convictions.

From Haman we learn: *Never underestimate the diabolical nature of revenge.* It will poison your life if you do. Proverbs says to "watch over your heart with all diligence, For from it flow the springs of life" (4:23). And if the source becomes poisoned, so will all the streams that flow out from it.

From the king we learn: *Never overestimate your own importance.* Some wise counselor should have come up alongside Ahasuerus and said to him, "What is this you're allowing? And why? Not even *you* are important enough to decide the fate of an entire nation!"

There have been or will be evil interludes in all of our lives. But we don't have to follow the script wickedness has written. We can break out of that role. We can change that tragic story line. But to do that we have to have Mordecai's courage behind our convictions to keep us from compromise.

 Living Insights STUDY ONE

It was Haman who plotted the destruction of the Jews—not God. So we should point the finger of blame not heavenward but heartward, for it was the wickedness in Haman's heart that engendered this great evil. As C. S. Lewis noted:

> When souls become wicked they will certainly use this possibility to hurt one another; and this, perhaps, accounts for four-fifths of the sufferings of men. It is men, not God, who have produced racks, whips, prisons, slavery, guns, bayonets, and bombs.[2]

---

2. C. S. Lewis, *The Problem of Pain* (reprint, New York, N.Y.: Macmillan Publishing Co., Collier Books, 1962), p. 89.

Proverbs has a lot to say about the wicked, usually in a context where they are contrasted with the righteous. Read through chapters 10–15 of that book, and jot down several of the verses that contrast the two.

Proverbs 10–15

Verse	Righteous	Wicked
10:3	The Lord will not allow the righteous to hunger	But He will thrust aside the craving of the wicked

Living Insights

As the Book of Esther contrasts righteous Mordecai with wicked Haman, so Psalm 1 contrasts the righteous and the wicked. Describe the image it uses to depict the righteous.

_____

_____

_____

The "streams of water" in verse 3 were not unattended natural streams, subject to flood and drought. They were man-made water canals dug near a reservoir to irrigate the farmer's garden. What does this tell you about how the righteous are cared for?

_____

_____

_____

Can you remember an example in your own life that illustrates God's protective care over your life?

_____

_____

_____

Describe the image used in the psalm to depict the wicked.

_____

_____

_____

Contrast this image with the one of the righteous.

_____

_____

_____

What is the destiny of the righteous?

_____

_____

What is the destiny of the wicked?

_____

_____

King Ahasuerus, at least at this point in our story, is walking in the counsel of the wicked Haman and sitting down to toast the fate of the Jews. If a blessing is conferred on those who *don't* walk in the counsel of the wicked, what could we expect to happen to the king if he continued down the path he was on?

_____

What path is your life taking—the path of the righteous or the path of the wicked? If you're headed the wrong way, just remember, God allows U-turns.

Chapter 5

THINKING, SAYING, AND DOING WHAT'S RIGHT— REGARDLESS

Esther 4

In a world of more than five billion people, it's easy to feel lost among the statistics. But you are not a number; you are unique (Ps. 139:13–14). There is no one quite like you in all the world. Even though you may *feel* insignificant from time to time, your life matters. As author Edward Everett Hale said:

> I am only one.
> But still I am one.
> I cannot do everything,
> But still I can do something;
> And because I cannot do everything
> I will not refuse to do the something that I can do.[1]

The Significant Impact of Only One

Both history and Scripture are full of people who thought like Edward Hale—people of conviction, people of courage, people who made a difference.

In History

Who can possibly measure the unending shadows cast by individuals who stood tall in their own lifetimes? Artists like da Vinci and Michelangelo. Military leaders like Lee, MacArthur, Eisenhower. Statesmen like Washington and Lincoln. Clergymen like Luther, Calvin, Wesley. Heroines like Joan of Arc, Madame Curie, Florence Nightingale, Amelia Earhart, Corrie ten Boom.

Of course, it may be argued that these were incredibly courageous individuals, gifted, geniuses, or people who held positions of highest rank. And you may be thinking, "What about little old me? What difference can *I* make?"

---

1. *Bartlett's Familiar Quotations*, 15th ed., rev. and enl., ed. Emily Morison Beck (Boston, Mass.: Little, Brown and Co., 1980), p. 590.

But one ordinary person can make a big difference. Just look at these examples.

> In 1776, One vote gave America the English language instead of German; . . .
> In 1845, One vote brought Texas into the Union;
> In 1868, One vote saved President Andrew Johnson from impeachment; . . .
> In 1876, One vote gave Rutherford B. Hayes the U.S. Presidency;
> In 1923, One vote gave Adolph Hitler control of the Nazi Party.[2]

In Scripture

The Bible is not a book that simply chronicles sweeping crusades or mass movements. It is the story of individuals—people like us. Ordinary people who decided to do something, to make a contribution, to stand up and be counted.

God, much more so than the marines, is looking for a few good men—and women.

> "For the eyes of the Lord move to and fro throughout the earth that He may strongly support those whose heart is completely His." (2 Chron. 16:9a)

> "And I searched for a man among them who should build up the wall and stand in the gap before Me for the land, that I should not destroy it; but I found no one." (Ezek. 22:30)

> They forgot God their Savior,
> Who had done great things in Egypt,
> Wonders in the land of Ham,
> And awesome things by the Red Sea.
> Therefore He said that He would destroy them,
> Had not Moses His chosen one stood in the breach before Him,
> To turn away His wrath from destroying them.
> (Ps. 106:21–23)

---

2. "One Vote," quoted by John Salisbury in "A Message for Americans," on KXL [Radio], Portland, Oregon. Multnomah County Republican Central Committee, April 1978.

In the last passage we see that Moses' intercession turned God's wrath away from destroying a rebellious generation. Moses couldn't do everything, but that didn't keep him from doing something. Nor did it keep Esther from doing something.

The Essential Intercession of Queen Esther

For Esther's people in Persia, life turned bleak overnight. Because of a wicked plan born in the anti-Semitic mind of Haman, every Jew in the nation was suddenly living on borrowed time. Before the year was out, their epitaphs would be chiseled in stone.

We see the diabolical plan set in motion in Esther 3:8–15. The capital city is thrown into a state of confusion; the atmosphere is one of bewilderment. Can this really be true? Can there be no appeal? Can there be anyone who could change the plan? Amend it? Delay it? Abolish it?

For the Jews, the sky was falling, and there was no place to hide.

Mourning and Weeping

The edict devastated the Jews. Every one of them who heard it cried out to God.

> When Mordecai learned all that had been done, he tore his clothes, put on sackcloth and ashes, and went out into the midst of the city and wailed loudly and bitterly. And he went as far as the king's gate, for no one was to enter the king's gate clothed in sackcloth. And in each and every province where the command and decree of the king came, there was great mourning among the Jews, with fasting, weeping, and wailing; and many lay on sackcloth and ashes. (Esther 4:1–3)

To this day people of Eastern cultures do not restrain their grief. Funeral processions are public times of loud wailing and weeping. No one hides their sorrow at tragic events, and Mordecai didn't either.

It was common in those days to wear loose-fitting, dark-colored, coarsely-woven garments made of goat's hair to signify repentance; sitting in a pile of ashes was a way of showing bitter remorse. So for Mordecai and the other Jews, doing these things was an acknowledgment that they were in utter ruin and that only God could restore them.

Esther, however, lived in another world, a world of silks and satins, sheltered from the sorrow in the street. That is, until news of her people's mourning reached her.

> Then Esther's maidens and her eunuchs came and told her, and the queen writhed in great anguish. (v. 4a)

Informing and Responding

Seeking a reliable source to explain this outburst of sorrow among her people, Esther sends a servant to question her cousin Mordecai.

> And she sent garments to clothe Mordecai that he might remove his sackcloth from him, but he did not accept them. Then Esther summoned Hathach from the king's eunuchs, whom the king had appointed to attend her, and ordered him to go to Mordecai to learn what this was and why it was. So Hathach went out to Mordecai to the city square in front of the king's gate. And Mordecai told him all that had happened to him, and the exact amount of money that Haman had promised to pay to the king's treasuries for the destruction of the Jews. He also gave him a copy of the text of the edict which had been issued in Susa for their destruction. (vv. 4b–8a)

In the verses, notice the following phrases: "*all* that happened" . . . "*exact* amount of money" . . . "a *copy* of the text of the edict." See how carefully Mordecai passes on the information to Esther? He doesn't hide the truth, but neither does he exaggerate. He doesn't estimate numbers; he is exact. He doesn't pass on rumors; he provides her with documented information.

Let's pause here for a moment of application. Are you that careful in passing along information? Are you able to document your stories? Do you make sure of the facts you're communicating?

Mordecai was careful to pass on accurate facts because he wanted the queen to be well informed. And he wanted her to be well informed because he wanted her to get involved. In fact, through Hathach he ordered her "to go in to the king to implore his favor and to plead with him for her people" (v. 8b).

Undergirding Mordecai's plea for Esther's involvement was the belief that one person *can* make a difference. But Esther churned at the request. Yes, there were her people to think about, but there was also her own life.

> Then Esther spoke to Hathach and ordered him to reply to Mordecai: "All the king's servants and the people of the king's provinces know that for any man or woman who comes to the king to the inner court who is not summoned, he has but one law, that he be put to death, unless the king holds out to him the golden scepter so that he may live. And I have not been summoned to come to the king for these thirty days." And they related Esther's words to Mordecai. (vv. 10–12)

Pleading and Praying

Upon hearing her response, Mordecai is faced with a dilemma. Should he back off or add pressure? With parental frankness, he sends a second appeal.

> Then Mordecai told them to reply to Esther, "Do not imagine that you in the king's palace can escape any more than all the Jews. For if you remain silent at this time, relief and deliverance will arise for the Jews from another place and you and your father's house will perish. And who knows whether you have not attained royalty for such a time as this?" (vv. 13–14)

Follow the lines of his reasoning: First, if you do nothing, sooner or later they will find out that you are a Jew and you, too, will be destroyed. Second, the Jewish race *will* survive, for God's promise to His people is greater than your willingness to be involved (Gen. 12:1–3)—if He has to, God will simply use someone else. Third, this turn of events could explain why you were elevated to such a high position.

Mordecai's power-packed rhetoric is reminiscent of one of the fiery speeches of Winston Churchill: "Let us . . . brace ourselves to our duties, and so bear ourselves that if the British Empire and its Commonwealth last for a thousand years, men will still say: 'This was their finest hour.' "[3]

3. *Bartlett's Familiar Quotations*, p. 744.

Esther has the same opportunity the British people had during World War II. If she chooses to stand, this could be her finest hour. Her decision? It's found in the very next verses.

> Then Esther told them to reply to Mordecai, "Go, assemble all the Jews who are found in Susa, and fast for me; do not eat or drink for three days, night or day. I and my maidens also will fast in the same way. And thus I will go in to the king, which is not according to the law; and if I perish, I perish." (Esther 4:15–16)

The king had chosen her to be queen on the basis of her beauty; God had chosen her on the basis of her character. And now her character rises to the occasion with heroic resolve: "If I perish, I perish."

The words are of the same spirit as Patrick Henry's "give me liberty or give me death!"[4] or as Nathan Hale's "I only regret that I have but one life to lose for my country."[5] But not only does Esther rise to heroism, but to leadership as well.

> So Mordecai went away and did just as Esther had commanded him. (v. 17)

Notice how Esther's entire outlook has shifted in the space of this chapter. From fear to faith. From reluctance to resolve. From concern for personal safety to the concern for the safety of her people. And from respect for Mordecai's leadership to the emergence of her own.

The Personal Involvement of Each Individual

As our world becomes more and more crowded, it's easy to feel lost in that crowd or to underestimate our significance. We wonder what difference we could possibly make in the spread of such sprawling issues as abortion, homelessness, crime, hunger, and drugs.

But one person *can* make a difference. Look at Mother Teresa or Billy Graham or James Dobson. Not until we believe this is true will we really be willing to risk. And only when we move from the safe harbor of theory to the rough waters of reality will we actually see any changes take place.

4. *Bartlett's Familiar Quotations*, p. 383.
5. *Bartlett's Familiar Quotations*, p. 401.

Do you really want to know how much difference one person can make? Scripture tells us that Jesus values one person so much that He's willing to leave the ninety-nine sheep that are safe and go after the one that is lost (see Luke 15:3–7). For no matter how big the fold, *one* is always a valuable number to God.

 ## Living Insights

What difference can a solitary life make? Consider the difference this one made two thousand years ago.

One Solitary Life

Here is a man who was born in an obscure village, the child of a peasant woman. He grew up in another obscure village. He worked in a carpenter shop until he was thirty, and then for three years he was an itinerant preacher. He never went to college. He never put his foot inside a big city. He never traveled two hundred miles from the place he was born. He never did one of the things that usually accompany greatness. He had no credentials but himself. He had nothing to do with this world except the naked power of his divine manhood.

While still a young man, the tide of public opinion turned against him. His friends ran away. One of them denied him. He was turned over to his enemies. He went through the mockery of a trial. He was nailed upon a cross between two thieves. His executioners gambled for the only piece of property He had on earth while He was dying, and that was His coat. When He was dead He was taken down and laid in a borrowed grave through the pity of a friend.

Nineteen wide centuries have come and gone, and today He is the centerpiece of the human race and leader of the column of progress.

I am far within the mark when I say that all the armies that ever marched, and all the navies that ever were built, and all the parliaments that ever sat, and all the kings that ever reigned, put together, have not affected the life of man upon this earth as powerfully as that One Solitary Life![6]

Write down a few ways Jesus' life has made a difference in yours.

_____

_____

_____

_____

_____

_____

 ## *Living Insights*

Consider another life that is making a difference today.

She is the most revered woman in the world. Mother Teresa's work among the dying on the streets of Calcutta is legendary. . . . Recipient of the Nobel Peace Prize for her world impact for good, Mother Teresa is an eloquent example of Christlike compassion.

Her indelible impact on the one-time enfant terrible of journalism, Malcolm Muggeridge, is recorded in his book, *Something Beautiful For God:* "In a dark time she is a burning and a shining light; in a cruel time, a living embodiment of Christ's gospel of love; in a godless time, the Word dwelling among us, full of grace and truth . . . All who have had the inestimable privilege of knowing her must be eternally grateful." . . .

"I am like a little pencil in His hand" she says of her ministry. "That is all. He does the thinking. He does the writing. The pencil has nothing to do with it. The pencil has only to be allowed to be used."[7]

---

6. [Phillips Brooks?] "One Solitary Life," quoted in *Behold the Man,* ed. Ralph L. Woods (New York, N.Y.: Macmillan Co., 1944), pp. 375–76.

7. "Something Beautiful for God," *The War Cry,* March 3, 1990, p. 2.

Consider one more solitary life—yours. What beautiful stories God could write if only you placed that little pencil in His hand. Won't you pray along in the following petition from Saint Francis of Assisi and yield your life to Him?

> Lord, make me an instrument of Your peace.
> Where there is hatred, let me sow love;
> Where there is injury, pardon;
> Where there is doubt, faith;
> Where there is despair, hope;
> Where there is darkness, light;
> And where there is sadness, joy.
>
> O Divine Master, grant that I may not
> So much seek to be consoled as to console;
> To be understood as to understand;
> To be loved as to love;
> For it is in giving that we receive;
> It is in pardoning that we are pardoned;
> And it is in dying
> That we are born to eternal life.[8]

8. Saint Francis of Assisi, quoted in *Every Knee Shall Bow,* comp. and ed. Joan Winmill Brown (Minneapolis, Minn.: Grason, 1978), p. 20.

Chapter 6

THE BEGINNING OF A COLLISION COURSE
Esther 5

Martin Luther took a stand against the most formidable power of his time—the Roman Catholic Church. He was like the Little Engine That Could going up against the entire Union-Pacific railroad.

In 1517 Luther called for a debate by nailing his Ninety-Five Theses on the Castle Church door in Wittenberg. This debate, along with his lectures and books, put him on a track that ran to Rome. A collision was inevitable.

In April of 1521 the governing council of the Germanic states convened in the city of Worms to confront Luther about his beliefs. When asked if he would repudiate his inflammatory statements about the Pope and the Church, he faced his accusers with stalwart resolve and proclaimed:

> I cannot and I will not recant anything . . . Here I stand. I cannot do otherwise. God help me. Amen.[1]

We saw this same type of resolve in Esther when she decided to stand alone against the most powerful man in Medo-Persia—her husband, the king.

> "And thus I will go in to the king, which is not according to the law; and if I perish, I perish." (Esther 4:16b)

Such courage is the mortar that martyrs are made of. It is also what cements our convictions so that we, like Luther and Esther, can stand up for our faith, even when we have to stand alone.

A Silent yet Powerful Interlude

Upon Mordecai's challenge, Esther didn't race immediately into the king's presence. Wisely, she waited, making a request of Mordecai first.

---

1. Martin Luther, quoted in *Here I Stand* by Roland H. Bainton (New York, N.Y.: New American Library of World Literature, Mentor Books, 1950), pp. 144–45.

"Go, assemble all the Jews who are found in Susa, and fast for me; do not eat or drink for three days, night or day." (v. 16a)

Mordecai obeyed Esther's command (v. 17); for three days the Jewish people fasted. During this time they calmed their emotions, gained perspective, and placed their problem in the hands of God—just as the prophet Isaiah advises in his book.

> Yet those who wait for the Lord
> Will gain new strength;
> They will mount up with wings like eagles,
> They will run and not get tired,
> They will walk and not become weary. (Isa. 40:31)

From this verse we learn of four things that happen when we wait on God rather than rush into a frenzy of activity. First, *we gain new strength*—which we'll need when the road gets rocky. Second, *we get a better perspective*—which gives us an eagle's eye view of our circumstances. Third, *we store up extra energy*—which we can draw upon at a later time. Fourth, *we deepen our determination to persevere* —which wards off weariness.

The bow atop this package of benefits is a sense of invincibility.

> "Do not fear, for I am with you;
> Do not anxiously look about you, for I am your God.
> I will strengthen you, surely I will help you,
> Surely I will uphold you with My righteous right hand.
> Behold, all those who are angered at you will be
>   shamed and dishonored;
> Those who contend with you will be as nothing,
>   and will perish.
> You will seek those who quarrel with you, but will
>   not find them,
> Those who war with you will be as nothing, and
>   non-existent.
> For I am the Lord your God, who upholds your right
>   hand,
> Who says to you, 'Do not fear, I will help you.'"
> (41:10–13)

Undoubtedly, these benefits of waiting strengthened Esther's resolve during her three-day fast. It was a silent yet powerful interlude in the queen's life.

A Calm yet Wise Plan

For three days Esther has waited on the Lord and gained new strength. Now it is time to test her wings.

> Now it came about on the third day that Esther put on her royal robes and stood in the inner court of the king's palace in front of the king's rooms, and the king was sitting on his royal throne in the throne room, opposite the entrance to the palace. And it happened when the king saw Esther the queen standing in the court, she obtained favor in his sight; and the king extended to Esther the golden scepter which was in his hand. So Esther came near and touched the top of the scepter. Then the king said to her, "What is troubling you, Queen Esther? And what is your request? Even to half of the kingdom it will be given to you." (Esther 5:1–3)

During times of prayer, fasting, and waiting, God prepares not only our hearts but the hearts of those who oppose us—even those who are unpredictable and hostile. See how softened the king's heart is toward Esther. In verse 2, "she obtained favor in his sight." In verse 3, he asked, "What is troubling you?"

Calmly, Esther unfolds the first step of her clever plan.

> And Esther said, "If it please the king, may the king and Haman come this day to the banquet that I have prepared for him." (v. 4)

Notice Esther's self-control. She doesn't spill out what's troubling her. She doesn't point a finger at Haman and ask for his head. She doesn't play on the king's emotions and manipulate him into action. She doesn't get into a frenzy, dissolve into tears, or act in haste. Instead, she sidesteps the question and issues an invitation.

Notice also that she has planned the banquet for that day. But wait—when would she have had time to prepare for such a party? During her three days of fasting. You see, waiting on the Lord doesn't mean we become inert. Even if we don't immerse ourselves in activity, we can still plan and prepare.

When the table is set and the moment is right, the issue of Esther's request comes up again.

> Then the king said, "Bring Haman quickly that we may do as Esther desires." So the king and Haman

came to the banquet which Esther had prepared. And, as they drank their wine at the banquet, the king said to Esther, "What is your petition, for it shall be granted to you. And what is your request? Even to half of the kingdom it shall be done." So Esther answered and said, "My petition and my request is: if I have found favor in the sight of the king, and if it please the king to grant my petition and do what I request, may the king and Haman come to the banquet which I shall prepare for them, and tomorrow I will do as the king says." (vv. 5–8)

Instead of answering the king's question, Esther invites him and Haman to still another banquet. Here the queen is a perfect example of peace and patience. She doesn't panic, because her confidence is not her own. Her waiting has produced in her an inner strength, that sense of invincibility we read about in Isaiah.

A Proud and Sinister Response

Suddenly the spotlight of the story turns onto Haman, the wicked official whose plan is to exterminate all the Jews. Notice his anger and arrogance in the following verses.

Then Haman went out that day glad and pleased of heart; but when Haman saw Mordecai in the king's gate, and that he did not stand up or tremble before him, Haman was filled with anger against Mordecai. Haman controlled himself, however, went to his house, and sent for his friends and his wife Zeresh. Then Haman recounted to them the glory of his riches, and the number of his sons, and every instance where the king had magnified him, and how he had promoted him above the princes and servants of the king. Haman also said, "Even Esther the queen let no one but me come with the king to the banquet which she had prepared; and tomorrow also I am invited by her with the king." (vv. 9–12)

It's easy to see what Haman's priorities were—the glory of his riches, the number of his sons, and the pride of his promotions.

What arrogance. He stands there preening himself, like a peacock spreading its iridescent feathers for all to admire. When a person is this self-absorbed, the focus is not on all those who bow down to him, but on the one who refuses to. That's why Mordecai grated on him so.

> "Yet all of this does not satisfy me every time I see Mordecai the Jew sitting at the king's gate." (v. 13)

Seeing how flustered Haman was, his wife came up with a solution that would keep Mordecai from spoiling her husband's dinner with the king.

> Then Zeresh his wife and all his friends said to him, "Have a gallows[2] fifty cubits high made and in the morning ask the king to have Mordecai hanged on it, then go joyfully with the king to the banquet." And the advice pleased Haman, so he had the gallows made. (v. 14)

Some Direct and Timely Advice

Woven into the fabric of our story today are four threads of advice. Let's unravel them one by one and knit them into our lives.

First, when preparing for an unprecedented event, wait on the Lord before getting involved.

Second, when dealing with an unpredictable person, count on the Lord to open the doors.

Third, when working through an unpleasant situation, trust the Lord for enduring patience.

Fourth, when standing against an unprincipled enemy, ask the Lord for invincible courage.

Our lesson today ends like the cliff-hangers of the old-time serials on the silent screen. Mordecai is about to be tied to the railroad track. Only Esther can save him. But will she rescue him in time? Will she thwart Haman's insidious plot to rid the empire of the Jewish people? At the risk of being melodramatic, all we can say is, "Tune in next time!"

---

2. The Hebrew word for *gallows* literally means "tree" or "pole." Apparently, it was not an elaborate structure but merely a tall pole.

Let's personalize the advice found at the end of our lesson.

Are you facing an unprecedented event in your life? Are you at a critical juncture where you need to decide or act or speak? If you are, try waiting before you do.

List the possible benefits of waiting in your particular case.

_____

_____

_____

_____

_____

Look up the following verses on waiting: Psalm 27:13–14, 37:34; Isaiah 26:8; Lamentations 3:25–26. Copy the verse that is most helpful to you in your present circumstances.

_____

_____

_____

Are you presently dealing with an unpredictable person? Here are some verses that may help you count on the Lord to open hearts and doors: Psalm 27:1–3; Proverbs 16:7, 21:1; Matthew 10:28–33. Copy the passage that helps you the most.

_____

_____

_____

_____

Are you working through an unpleasant situation? Are you having difficulty trusting the Lord for enduring patience? If so, maybe these verses will help: Job 13:15, 23:10; James 1:2–3; 1 Peter 4:12–19. Of those, copy the one that most helps you to trust.

Are you standing against an unprincipled enemy? Are your knees knocking for fear of what might happen to you? What you need is invincible courage. See if these verses don't help: 1 Samuel 17:45, 2 Kings 6:15–17, Psalm 18:1–3, Romans 8:31. Copy the passage that most strengthens your heart.

 ## Living Insights

Probably more than any other person in the Bible, David knew what it was like to face unprecedented events, to deal with unpredictable people, to work through unpleasant situations, and to stand against unprincipled enemies.

Through the furnace of these experiences, David learned to wait, to count on the Lord for deliverance, to trust Him for patience, and to ask Him for invincible courage.

The book of Psalms is the gold that came out of the furnace of the fiery ordeals David endured. We have chosen a few psalms that represent the different problems David faced in his turbulent life. Psalm 18 is when he had to face an unprecedented event. Psalm 62 is when he dealt with unpredictable people. Psalm 116 is when he worked through an unpleasant situation. Psalm 37 is when he stood against unprincipled enemies. Pick one of these psalms and study it. Write your observations.

_____

_____

_____

_____

_____

_____

_____

_____

Jot down a few of the key verses in this psalm that offer particular encouragement to you in your present circumstances.

_____

_____

_____

_____

_____

_____

_____

Personalize the psalm by reading your circumstances into it, and then pray the psalm back to God.

Chapter 7

TURNABOUT IS FAIR PLAY

Esther 6

Things are not always as they seem. Case in point:

A shipwrecked man was once washed ashore on an uninhabited island. In the days that followed he painstakingly constructed a hut with a few things he salvaged from the wreck and from whatever he could find on the island. That little hut was the only protection he had from the harsh elements and the only place he could safeguard his possessions.

Upon returning one evening from a lengthy search for food, he was terrified to find the hut engulfed in flames. The loss devastated him. He spent that night despondent, sleeping on the sand.

He awoke early the next morning and, to his surprise, saw a ship anchored off the island. A crew member stepped ashore and told him, "We saw your smoke signal and came to rescue you!"

What seemed to be destruction turned out to be deliverance. And such was the case with Mordecai. He had been shipwrecked by an anti-Semitic undercurrent on an island of injustice, and now he stood in death's shadow. Every hope that sheltered him seemed to have gone up in smoke.

But then, as we will find out today, things are not always as they seem.

When All Seems Lost, It Isn't

For the Jews living in Persia in Mordecai's time, it seemed as if all was lost. First, their protection seemed lost. They had no advocate except for the queen. But how powerful was she in the shadow of the king? Second, their future seemed lost. The sand in the hourglass was rapidly running out. Genocide seemed inevitable. It was just a matter of time. As a result, their hope seemed lost.

Yet in spite of the way things seemed, that's not the way things were. Behind the scenes God was at work. His providential plan to deliver the Jews was being enacted by Esther. The king had given her not only an audience but also *carte blanche* to request anything she desired, up to half his kingdom.

None of the Jews, though, knew what was happening behind the palace doors. Not even Haman knew. He was too busy building the gallows for his nemesis Mordecai to know anything but his own desire for revenge.

How Mordecai must have brooded as the pole for his execution was raised. How ominously it stood, like a cruel scepter raised in judgment over his life.

It would have been easy for Mordecai to curl up and lick his wounds, to bemoan the fact that no one noticed how he had once saved the king but was now being treated unjustly.

This brings us to the second principle.

When No One Seems to Notice, God Does

Just when the shadow of death seemed darkest, a ray of hope shone from the king's chambers.

> During that night the king could not sleep so he gave an order to bring the book of records, the chronicles, and they were read before the king. And it was found written what Mordecai had reported concerning Bigthana and Teresh, two of the king's eunuchs who were doorkeepers, that they had sought to lay hands on King Ahasuerus. And the king said, "What honor or dignity has been bestowed on Mordecai for this?" Then the king's servants who attended him said, "Nothing has been done for him." (Esther 6:1–3)

Often momentous events hang upon the slenderest of threads. Here the deliverance of the Jews was precipitated by something as insignificant as insomnia. While all of Susa slept, the king lay awake—a reminder that God is not distant or indifferent. He sees. He cares. He intervenes on our behalf.

While the king tossed and turned, Mordecai slept. Another reminder—that God watches over His beloved even while they sleep (Ps. 127:2). So in spite of the fact that no one seems to notice, God does. That's as true in our day as it was in Mordecai's. Though we may feel abandoned, we are never out of God's watchful eye or far from His protective care.

As a soporific, the king ordered his staff to read him to sleep. But in their reading, he found himself suddenly alert instead of slowly anesthetized. The reason was the story of an aborted assassination plot, foiled by a man named Mordecai. The incident is chronicled earlier in Esther.

> In those days, while Mordecai was sitting at the king's gate, Bigthan and Teresh, two of the king's officials from those who guarded the door, became angry and sought to lay hands on King Ahasuerus. But the plot became known to Mordecai, and he told Queen Esther, and Esther informed the king in Mordecai's name. Now when the plot was investigated and found to be so, they were both hanged on a gallows; and it was written in the Book of the Chronicles in the king's presence. (Esther 2:21–23)

Are you a modern-day Mordecai? Have your accomplishments been overlooked? Have the promotions and the perks gone to someone else when it was you responsible for the success of a project? Have others been given the credit that was due you? If so, learn a lesson from Mordecai. Don't become resentful and don't entertain revenge. Trust God—instead of taking justice into your own hands.

> For God is not unjust so as to forget your work and the love which you have shown toward His name, in having ministered and in still ministering to the saints. (Heb. 6:10)

When no one seems to notice, remember, God does (compare Matt. 6:3–4 with Mark 12:41–44).

This brings us to our next principle.

When Everything Seems Great, It's Not

As soon as the king heard that nothing had been done to reward Mordecai, he immediately set out to rectify the situation. And he sought advice, ironically, from the person whose agenda for Mordecai was diametrically opposed to his.

> So the king said, "Who is in the court?" Now Haman had just entered the outer court of the king's palace in order to speak to the king about hanging Mordecai on the gallows which he had prepared for him. And the king's servants said to him, "Behold, Haman is standing in the court." And the king said, "Let him

come in." So Haman came in and the king said to him, "What is to be done for the man whom the king desires to honor?" (Esther 6:4–6a)

The king's question started the wheels turning in Haman's mind. Thinking that he was the one the king wanted to honor, Haman let his greedy imagination run free.

> And Haman said to himself, "Whom would the king desire to honor more than me?" Then Haman said to the king, "For the man whom the king desires to honor, let them bring a royal robe which the king has worn, and the horse on which the king has ridden, and on whose head a royal crown has been placed; and let the robe and the horse be handed over to one of the king's most noble princes and let them array the man whom the king desires to honor and lead him on horseback through the city square, and proclaim before him, 'Thus it shall be done to the man whom the king desires to honor.'" (vv. 6b–9)

Boy, was Haman in for a surprise! You could almost hear his jaw hit the floor when the king unveiled the person of honor.

> Then the king said to Haman, "Take quickly the robes and the horse as you have said, and do so for Mordecai the Jew, who is sitting at the king's gate; do not fall short in anything of all that you have said." (v. 10)

How ironic—the very man champing to hang Mordecai was the one chosen to honor him.

> So Haman took the robe and the horse, and arrayed Mordecai, and led him on horseback through the city square, and proclaimed before him, "Thus it shall be done to the man whom the king desires to honor." (v. 11)

Two more contrasting characters than these could not be placed alongside one another. One sat upon a regal horse, robed in royal attire. The other walked before him, proclaiming his praise. The words must have lodged in Haman's throat. How humiliated he must have felt . . . and how infuriated.

Yet Mordecai remained unaffected by all the pomp and praise. How do we know this? Look at the next verse.

Then Mordecai returned to the king's gate. (v. 12a)

Where we find Mordecai, when all the laudatory dust settles, is back where he started—at the king's gate (see v. 10). Have you been suddenly promoted to a place of prominence or praise? If so, learn a lesson from Mordecai.

> A proud ambitious man would have said to himself, "No more of the king's gate for me! I shall direct my steps now to the king's palace, and hold myself ready for honour . . . which surely must now be at hand." Mordecai seems to have said with himself, "*If* these things are designed for me in God's good providence, they will find me. But they must seek me, for I shall not seek them. Those who confer them know my address. 'Mordecai at the king's gate,' will still find me. Let the crowd wonder and disperse. I have had enough of their incense. Let Haman go whither he will, he is in the hands of the Lord. Let my friends at home wait; they will hear all in time. . . . I can wait best at the old place and in the accustomed way—'at the king's gate.'"[1]

When Nothing Seems Just, It Is

It has been said that "the mills of God grind slowly, yet they grind exceedingly small."[2] Haman found himself to be but tiny grist in those mills. His life was under judgment, and it was just a matter of time before the mills of providence would grind his bones to dust.

No longer preening like a peacock, Haman slinked home like a whipped dog, his tail tucked between his legs. He was a beaten man.

> But Haman hurried home, mourning, with his head covered. And Haman recounted to Zeresh his wife and all his friends everything that had happened to him. Then his wise men and Zeresh his wife said to

1. Alexander Raleigh, *Book of Esther* (1880; reprint, Minneapolis, Minn.: Klock and Klock Christian Publishers, 1980), pp. 155–56.

2. Henry Wadsworth Longfellow, quoted in *The Home Book of Quotations*, 10th ed., comp. Burton Stevenson (New York, N.Y.: Dodd, Mead and Co., 1967), p. 1708.

him, "If Mordecai, before whom you have begun to fall, is of Jewish origin, you will not overcome him, but will surely fall before him." (vv. 12b–13)

The warning from Haman's wife appears to be something of a muted echo from Genesis 12:2–3, where God said to Abraham:

"And I will make you a great nation,
And I will bless you, . . .
And I will bless those who bless you,
And the one who curses you I will curse."[3]
(emphasis added)

Almost before his wife's words could sink in, Haman was whisked off to the royal banquet. Doubtless, his head spun as he ascended the palace steps.

While they were still talking with him, the king's eunuchs arrived and hastily brought Haman to the banquet which Esther had prepared. (Esther 6:14)

We would have warned Haman as he went to the banquet, What goes around comes around. For little did he know that the fateful course he had planned to cater for Mordecai was about to be dished out to him instead.

In Conclusion

We have seen four facets of our lesson's principle: *Things are not always as they seem.*

1. When all seems lost, it isn't.
2. When no one seems to notice, God does.
3. When everything seems great, it's not.
4. When nothing seems just, it is.

All this is a long way of saying that even when God seems absent, He is there. In sickness or health. In poverty or prosperity. In promotion or demotion. In the darkest night or the brightest day. He is there, watching, waiting, and working at the slow but sure mills of providence, grinding out His will both upon the wheat and upon the chaff . . . upon the Mordecais as well as upon the Hamans of this world.

---

3. The last clause literally means, "I will bind under a curse."

Living Insights

During the arrest, trial, and crucifixion of Christ, things were not as they seemed. It seemed as if Jesus was on His way to defeat. In reality, He was on His way to victory. All seemed dark and hopeless when the cross was shrouded in darkness. But on that first Easter morning, hope dawned triumphantly to herald a risen Savior.

Think through the Scriptures and see if you can come up with other examples that illustrate the four facets of the principle, *Things are not always as they seem.*

- When all seems lost, it isn't.

_____

_____

_____

- When no one seems to notice, God does.

_____

_____

_____

- When everything seems great, it's not.

_____

_____

_____

- When nothing seems just, it is.

_____

_____

_____

If you need a little help in jogging your memory, read through Hebrews 11.

In C. S. Lewis' *The Screwtape Letters*, the warning that a senior devil gives to a fledgling demon is both poignant and practical.

> Our cause is never more in danger than when a human, no longer desiring, but still intending, to do our Enemy's will, looks round upon a universe from which every trace of Him seems to have vanished, and asks why he has been forsaken, and still obeys.[4]

It's important to understand that if we live our lives by the way things appear, we are living by sight rather than by faith (see 2 Cor. 5:7). What would have happened to the Jewish race if Esther and Mordecai had lived that way? A little closer to home, what would happen to you if you simply lived by the way things appeared?

Reflect on times in your life when appearances displayed a deceptive front. Try to remember specific situations that illustrate the four facets of the principle, *Things are not always as they seem.*

- When all seems lost, it isn't.

  _____

  _____

  _____

- When no one seems to notice, God does.

  _____

  _____

  _____

- When everything seems great, it's not.

  _____

  _____

  _____

---

4. C. S. Lewis, *The Screwtape Letters* (reprint, New York, N.Y.: Macmillan Publishing Co., 1961), p. 39.

- When nothing seems just, it is.

_____

_____

_____

To help you through the next series of mirages Satan may throw your way, write Habakkuk 3:17–19 on a three-by-five-inch card and commit it to memory. More importantly, commit yourself to it.

> Though the fig tree should not blossom,
> And there be no fruit on the vines,
> Though the yield of the olive should fail,
> And the fields produce no food,
> Though the flock should be cut off from the fold,
> And there be no cattle in the stalls,
> Yet I will exult in the Lord,
> I will rejoice in the God of my salvation.
> The Lord God is my strength,
> And He has made my feet like hinds' feet,
> And makes me walk on my high places.

Chapter 8
ULTIMATE POETIC JUSTICE
Esther 7

*P*oetic justice is "a term introduced into England by Thomas Rymer in 1678, denoting the reward of the virtuous and the punishment of the vicious. . . . that all characters reap the harvest of their just deserts."[1]

As Christians, we believe that ultimate poetic justice will be meted out at the judgment seat of Christ (2 Cor. 5:10). Until that time, however, we must live with injustice and the silence of heaven's gavel.

Job is a perfect example of someone who not only lived with injustice but wrestled with it. Though godly in heart and righteous in life, Job became the object of supernatural cruelty.

Like a large cat with a tiny, wounded mouse, Satan played havoc with the man, leaving him homeless, helpless, and hurting. But the presence of pain was not the hardest part of Job's trial; instead, it was the absence of God.

There was no voice from heaven—only silence. It was as if God had turned His back on His faithful friend, refusing to look as Job suffered.

It must have been like swimming in a large lake at dusk when a thick fog rolls in. Within seconds, you can see nothing—no horizon, no landmarks, no lights along the shore. You lose all sense of direction. You panic and start swimming in one direction. Then you turn to swim in another. Finally, with your heart pounding, you realize the only thing to do is to tread water and wait for a voice from the shore to orient you.

Undoubtedly, Esther and Mordecai both found themselves enveloped in a fog that muffled the voice of God. All who have suffered the silence of God amidst the presence of injustice can understand their disoriented feelings. The fog is bad enough, but the silence from the shore is unbearable.

---

1. *A Dictionary of Literary Terms*, comp. Sylvan Barnet, Morton Berman, and William Burto (Boston, Mass.: Little, Brown and Co., 1960; London, England: Constable and Co., 1964), see "poetic justice."

Although God is just, He is just in His own time. And in between the ticks of His pocket watch are gaps of silence. Sometimes inexplicable silence.

Understanding God's Timing in Our Day

In order to understand the enigma of God's silence, we have to understand the difference between our time and God's, between Earthly Standard Time and Heavenly Mountain Time.

Our Time

Part of trying to reconcile these time zones is understanding that here on earth we are prisoners of a cage called Time. God exists outside that cage, unfettered by the constrictions we must live with, day in, day out.

For us, time is objectively measured. For the day, we look at our watches. For the week, we turn to our schedules. For the year, we consult our calendars. Everything we measure is from this present moment. That is our constant orientation.

For us, time is consciously accountable. Events are seen, visible. We can even capture them on videotape. The objects involved are tangible; we can touch them, feel them. And people are present, witnessing what's said and done.

For us, time is rarely ignored. Only when we sleep or daydream do we escape from time. Yet even then we cannot escape entirely. Our jaunt is only mental; physically, we're still captive.

None of the above is true for God. Although we are trapped in the ever-present Now, God is free from the trammels of time.

God's Time

God is not bound by wristwatches and wall calendars. His time is *infinitely immeasurable.* And because He transcends time itself, His time is *absolutely intangible.*

We see history as a sequence of still frames, viewed one after another, as in a motion picture reel. But God sees the entire movie at once. That is why He can remain silent in act 1 of the drama of our lives—because He knows how the final act will turn out. As author of this epic drama called Life, He knows that ultimately justice will win out, that good will triumph over evil, and that all the loose ends will be tied up in His grand denouement.

No matter how we rationalize, God will sometimes *seem* unfair from the perspective of a person trapped in time. Only at the end of time, after we have attained God's level of viewing, after every evil has been punished or forgiven, every illness healed, and the entire universe restored—only then will fairness reign. Then we will understand what role is played by evil, and by the Fall, and by natural law, in an "unfair" event like the death of a child. Until then, we will not know, and can only trust in a God who does know.

We remain ignorant of many details, not because God enjoys keeping us in the dark, but because we have not the faculties to absorb so much light. At a single glance God knows what the world is about and how history will end. But we time-bound creatures have only the most primitive manner of understanding: we can let time pass. Not until history has run its course will we understand how "all things work together for good." Faith means believing in advance what will only make sense in reverse.[2]

Discovering God's Timing in Esther's Day

We love to sing the hymn,

> In His time, in His time;
> He makes all things beautiful in His time.
> Lord, please show me ev'ry day
> As You're teaching me Your way,
> That You do just what You say in Your time.[3]

Yet the words are harder to sing without divine accompaniment. When there are no notes from heaven to cue us and keep us on key, it's difficult to sing that song. Sure, we can lip-sync the lyrics, but the tune is really not in our hearts, is it?

A Sustained Period of Silence

How difficult it must have been for Esther and Mordecai to sing those stanzas a cappella. When the king promoted Haman, God

2. Philip Yancey, *Disappointment with God* (Grand Rapids, Mich.: Zondervan Publishing House, 1988), pp. 200–201.

3. Diane Ball, "In His Time" (Laguna Hills, Calif.: Maranatha! Music, 1978). Used by permission.

stayed silent (Esther 3:1). When Haman plotted to destroy the Jews, God stayed silent (3:6). When the king made an agreement with Haman, God stayed silent (3:9–11). When Mordecai pleaded with the queen to intervene, God stayed silent (chap. 4). When Haman ordered gallows built for Mordecai, God stayed silent (5:14).

The silence of God is deafening in the Book of Esther. But there are other places in Scripture where we strain to hear a word from heaven and hear none. Think of the four hundred years of silence that yawn between the books of Genesis and Exodus. The time of Samuel's birth when word from the Lord was rare and visions were infrequent (1 Sam. 3:1). The frustrating silence that Habakkuk had to endure (Hab. 1:2–4). The four-hundred-year silence between the testaments, bookended by Malachi and Matthew. The silence of heaven when Jesus hung on the cross (Mark 15:34).

Maybe you're experiencing a similar enigma: How could God be so silent when I cry out to Him so loudly, so desperately? Why doesn't He answer? Why doesn't He call out from the shore so I can orient myself in the fog that has enveloped me?

If you find yourself treading water in that foggy lake, there's an important thing you need to remember: *The periods of God's silence are just as significant as the times He speaks.* It is during such times that the ears of our faith become fine-tuned.

A Subtle Turn of Events

In chapter 6 of Esther, we saw that a subtle but pivotal turn of events had taken place. The king couldn't sleep, so he had his servants read the historical records to him. But instead of curing his insomnia, the reading braced him like a pot of hot coffee. The mention of Mordecai's heroism prompted the king to honor this unsung hero. The irony of it all was that the king appointed Haman, Mordecai's sworn enemy, to herald Mordecai's praise. When Haman returned home from this humiliating parade, he heard a different tune from his wife and friends than the one he had heard before. It was as if one day Haman had come home to a festive dance, while the next, to a funeral dirge.

As we stand back and observe this subtle turn of events, we sense that something more is brewing. Amidst the silence, we sense the deeper stirring of God's sovereignty.

A Sudden Change in Plans

These events in chapter 6 usher us into a second banquet in chapter 7.

> Now the king and Haman came to drink wine
> with Esther the queen. And the king said to Esther
> on the second day also as they drank their wine at
> the banquet, "What is your petition, Queen Esther?
> It shall be granted you. And what is your request?
> Even to half of the kingdom it shall be done."
> (vv. 1–2)

This is the third time the king has asked Esther about her petition (see 5:3, 6). Between the time of the first banquet and this one, God inserted an important parenthesis. He revealed to the king how Mordecai had saved his life, which prompted the king to honor this loyal and courageous man.

The delay between the first and second banquets was deliberate, both on Esther's part and on God's. God wasn't late, nor was He negligent. He was synchronizing the events of His sovereign plan to come together at just the right time for optimal effect. In delaying her request until the second banquet, Esther was being sensitive to God's timing. She was careful not to rush things but to take everything "in His time."

At the table, Esther finally voices her petition. As she speaks, Haman sits in a paralyzed silence, the echo of his wife's words still ringing in his ears (see 6:13b).

> Then Queen Esther answered and said, "If I have
> found favor in your sight, O king, and if it please
> the king, let my life be given me as my petition,
> and my people as my request; for we have been sold,
> I and my people, to be destroyed, to be killed and
> to be annihilated. Now if we had only been sold as
> slaves, men and women, I would have remained si-
> lent, for the trouble would not be commensurate with
> the annoyance to the king." Then King Ahasuerus
> asked Queen Esther, "Who is he, and where is he,
> who would presume to do thus?" And Esther said,
> "A foe and an enemy, is this wicked Haman!" Then
> Haman became terrified before the king and queen.
> (7:3–6)

A Surprising Climax

When Esther said his name, Haman probably dropped his goblet. In verses 7–10 the drama reaches its climax in a gripping scene of ultimate poetic justice.

And the king arose in his anger from drinking wine and went into the palace garden; but Haman stayed to beg for his life from Queen Esther, for he saw that harm had been determined against him by the king. Now when the king returned from the palace garden into the place where they were drinking wine, Haman was falling on the couch where Esther was. Then the king said, "Will he even assault the queen with me in the house?" As the word went out of the king's mouth, they covered Haman's face. Then Harbonah, one of the eunuchs who were before the king said, "Behold indeed, the gallows standing at Haman's house fifty cubits high, which Haman made for Mordecai who spoke good on behalf of the king!" And the king said, "Hang him on it." So they hanged Haman on the gallows which he had prepared for Mordecai, and the king's anger subsided.

Being Sensitive to God's Interventions Every Day

If you find yourself thrashing about in a lake covered with fog, or maybe just dog-paddling with your head barely above the water-line, here are a few things to remember.

- *The fog on your lake is neither accidental nor fatal.* Be careful not to make so much noise trying to keep afloat that you can't hear the voice from the shore. While swimming, listen for His voice. It will come in various ways, so you must be open to hearing it, intent on hearing it, and sensitive to its sound. It is the voice of God piercing the fog that gives you the assurance that your circumstances are neither accidental nor fatal.

- *The workings of our God are related to our crises but unrelated to our clocks.* While waiting, look beyond the present. You'll be amazed how it will help you bear the pain.

- *The surprises in store are not merely ironic or coincidental; they are sovereignly designed.* While anticipating them, trust Him for justice. Guard against the temptation to question the integrity of the Judge or to impugn His motives.

Esther and Mordecai are not the only Old Testament characters who found themselves in a fog with zero visibility. Jeremiah is another. He is known as the weeping prophet, and his tears are recorded in the book of Lamentations. His words are cast in the form of a funeral dirge because he was mourning the destruction of Jerusalem and the captivity of the Jewish people.

Read through the lyrics of his mournful song, and write down some of the verses of doubt and disillusionment that you identify with.

Verse   **Why Do You Identify with It?**

_____   _____

_____   _____

_____   _____

_____   _____

_____   _____

_____   _____

_____   _____

Write down the verse that reflects the turning point in Jeremiah's perspective on his pain.

_____

_____

_____

_____

Now jot down some of the verses in Lamentations that speak to you like that voice from the shore, which we talked about in our lesson.

_____

_____

_____

_____

_____

_____

_____

_____

 ## *Living Insights*

In his excellent book *Waiting: Finding Hope When God Seems Silent,* Ben Patterson concludes with these words. Let's take time to meditate on them.

> The prayer that wrestles with the living God has the faith to believe in the end that even the apparent silence of God is the silence of his higher thoughts and that his no is spoken that he might give us a more resounding yes.
>
> There is a lovely poem which speaks to this wonderfully. It was reputedly written by a young soldier who received massive and permanently debilitating injuries in the Civil War. He lived as a cripple the rest of his days, wrestling and waiting for God to show his face, his purpose in it all. At the end of his strugglings, he wrote this:
>
> I asked for strength that I might achieve;
> > I was made weak that I might obey.
> I asked for health that I might do greater things;
> > I was given infirmity that I might do better things.
> I asked for riches that I might be happy;
> > I was given poverty that I might be wise.
> I asked for power that I might have the praise of men;
> > I was given weakness that I might feel the need of God.
> I asked for all things that I might enjoy life;
> > I was given life that I might enjoy all things.

I have received nothing I asked for, all that
I hoped for.
My prayer is answered.
Such sentiments can be expressed, not at the beginning of our struggle with God, but only at the end.
It is a precious intimacy with the heart of God that
can see through all of our disappointments the tender and loving hand of God at work for our good.
That intimacy comes only after years spent in dialog
with him, a dialog that is sometimes quiet and peaceful and sometimes wrenching and devastating. But
through it all there is the same loving God, no matter how we feel him to be at the moment—adversary
or advocate, mother or father, friend or enemy.
Through it all he is at work for our good, and his
victory over us will be also his victory in us when
the wrestling is over.[4]

4. Ben Patterson, *Waiting: Finding Hope When God Seems Silent* (Downers Grove, Ill.: Inter-Varsity Press, 1989), pp. 147–48.

Chapter 9

AND THE WALL
CAME TUMBLING DOWN

Esther 8

Some walls seem set in concrete and impossible to budge. But if history teaches us anything, it teaches that no matter how intimidating or long-standing, every wall will ultimately fall.

The ruins of ancient walls are strewn amid the rubble of crumbled empires. Egypt. Greece. Rome. All were once imposing world powers whose cities were protected by formidable walls. Now they are simply scenic spots brought to life by travel brochures and tour guides.

No wall looms as dramatically in our minds as the Berlin wall. For twenty-eight years it divided East and West Berlin, communism and capitalism. It stretched across the city like an ugly gash, its barbed wire forming cruel stitches. Its great masses of concrete seemed immovable.

But on November 9, 1989, the wall started to crumble. It collapsed without one shot being fired.

Jericho's wall was similarly imposing. But through a small band of men who were willing to trust God for impossible things, that wall also came tumbling down (Josh. 6:20).

Other walls, though less tangible, sometimes appear equally impossible to budge. The wall of a critical spirit. The wall of a stubborn will. The wall of an offended friend.

The eighth chapter of Esther is going to teach us some valuable lessons about walls and how to overcome them—even those that appear impenetrable.

Whether you're facing a Berlin wall or a wall around someone's heart, remember—there is no wall so strong that God is not stronger still.

Walls that Fell in Esther's Day

There is no scene so dark that God cannot brighten it. There is no writing so permanent that He cannot change it. And there is no heart so hard that He cannot soften it. Even if that heart resides in the most powerful person on earth.

An Unchangeable Heart

King Ahasuerus had a vast empire (Esther 1:1–2). His word was law, which gave him absolute power over his people. This same influential man had promoted the Jew-hater, Haman (3:1), who then devised a plan to exterminate all the Jews in the empire, a plan that the king ratified (3:8–9a, 11). And yet, in Esther 8:1–4, we witness an absolutely amazing thing.

> On that day King Ahasuerus gave the house of Haman, the enemy of the Jews, to Queen Esther; and Mordecai came before the king, for Esther had disclosed what he was to her. And the king took off his signet ring which he had taken away from Haman, and gave it to Mordecai. And Esther set Mordecai over the house of Haman.
>
> Then Esther spoke again to the king, fell at his feet, wept, and implored him to avert the evil scheme of Haman the Agagite and his plot which he had devised against the Jews. And the king extended the golden scepter to Esther. So Esther arose and stood before the king.

The king's heart had changed from one that gave the Jews into Haman's hands to one that gave Haman's estate into the hands of two Jews. The walls around a person's heart *can* come down, no matter how high, how hard, or how long they've been there.

> The king's heart is like channels of water in the
> hand of the Lord;
> He turns it wherever He wishes.
> (Prov. 21:1)

No heart is so hard that God cannot break through it. And if He wants to tear down a wall, it doesn't matter whether that person is your boss, your mate, your neighbor, or the king of the Medo-Persian Empire.

An Irrevocable Edict

Although the king's heart has softened and Haman has been put to death, another wall still stands that Esther must confront—the royal edict that is still in effect.

> Then she said, "If it pleases the king and if I have found favor before him and the matter seems proper

to the king and I am pleasing in his sight, let it be written to revoke the letters devised by Haman, the son of Hammedatha the Agagite, which he wrote to destroy the Jews who are in all the king's provinces. For how can I endure to see the calamity which shall befall my people, and how can I endure to see the destruction of my kindred?" So King Ahasuerus said to Queen Esther and to Mordecai the Jew, "Behold, I have given the house of Haman to Esther, and him they have hanged on the gallows because he had stretched out his hands against the Jews. Now you write to the Jews as you see fit, in the king's name, and seal it with the king's signet ring; for a decree which is written in the name of the king and sealed with the king's signet ring may not be revoked." (Esther 8:5–8)

The king's response was extraordinary, especially in light of the law of the Medo-Persians that makes royal edicts irrevocable (compare Dan. 6:8, 12, 15). And yet that wall crumbled in the face of yet another edict.

So the king's scribes were called at that time in the third month (that is, the month Sivan), on the twenty-third day; and it was written according to all that Mordecai commanded to the Jews, the satraps, the governors, and the princes of the provinces which extended from India to Ethiopia, 127 provinces, to every province according to its script, and to every people according to their language, as well as to the Jews according to their script and their language. And he wrote in the name of King Ahasuerus, and sealed it with the king's signet ring, and sent letters by couriers on horses, riding on steeds sired by the royal stud. In them the king granted the Jews who were in each and every city the right to assemble and to defend their lives, to destroy, to kill, and to annihilate the entire army of any people or province which might attack them, including children and women, and to plunder their spoil, on one day in all the provinces of King Ahasuerus, the thirteenth day of the twelfth month (that is, the month Adar).

> A copy of the edict to be issued as law in each and
> every province, was published to all the peoples, so
> that the Jews should be ready for this day to avenge
> themselves on their enemies. The couriers, hastened
> and impelled by the king's command, went out, rid-
> ing on the royal steeds; and the decree was given
> out in Susa the capital. (Esther 8:9–14)

Since the edict of Haman could not be revoked, the king allowed
Esther and Mordecai to draft a separate edict. Their edict did not
annul the first one, per se, but it effectively annulled it by giving
the Jews the right not only to defend themselves but to take severe
retaliatory action. This countermeasure put fear in the enemies of
the Jews and averted genocide.

Can you identify with the Jews living under the edict of extermination? Have you felt the cold, hard wall that some powerful person
has erected around you, isolating and intimidating you? The bricks
of that wall may have been letters or lawsuits or libelous statements
in the newspaper. They may have been slurs against your reputation
or slander against your character. They may have left you crumbled
in a helpless heap, bruised and broken, with your bleeding fists
pounding against that wall.

If so, this paragraph in Esther 8 should come as an edict of
encouragement. Murderous indictments can be neutralized. What
seems permanent can be amended, even nullified, by the counter-
measures of God.

An Impenetrable Gloom

Although Haman was dead, to the Jews his shadow still loomed
menacingly across the land. Their days were numbered. They were
marked people, targets for destruction. And they were living in a
death-row atmosphere of impenetrable gloom.

That is, until they received that second edict.

> Then Mordecai went out from the presence of
> the king in royal robes of blue and white, with a
> large crown of gold and a garment of fine linen and
> purple; and the city of Susa shouted and rejoiced.
> For the Jews there was light and gladness and joy
> and honor. And in each and every province, and in
> each and every city, wherever the king's command-
> ment and his decree arrived, there was gladness and

joy for the Jews, a feast and a holiday. And many among the peoples of the land became Jews, for the dread of the Jews had fallen on them. (vv. 15–17)

Walls that Fall on Any Day

The walls in Jericho, Medo-Persia, and Berlin seemed immovable. Yet they fell. And their collapse was felt throughout the world. The walls that fall in our own lives may not send tremors across the earth, but they, nonetheless, can seem to be equally formidable obstacles and equally frustrating to overcome.

We're not talking about bricks and barbed wire or mortar and masonry. We're talking about the walls of stubborn wills, the walls of slanderous statements, the walls of depression and doom. Walls we all run into, some on a daily basis. Walls that dwarf and discourage us.

No matter how stubborn the will that opposes you, just remember, "Greater is He who is in you than he who is in the world" (1 John 4:4). If God truly is for you, whose will—regardless of how stubborn—can oppose you (Rom. 8:31)?

The example from Esther should be of real encouragement to us. When things seem unchangeable, they're not. God can tear down the walls of a stubborn heart just as easily as those of a fortified empire.

Maybe, though, the wall that towers above your life is not a stubborn will but a slanderous statement. Maybe it's a damaging document or a juicy morsel of gossip that's being passed around. If so, remember the edict of Haman. Even though it seemed irrevocable, it wasn't. The edict from Esther and Mordecai, in effect, annulled it. And God can do that for you with a word or a letter of defense from someone who believes in you.

Perhaps, though, the wall that surrounds you is not a stubborn will or a damaging document. It may be a wall of depression and doom instead. Even though those feelings seem impenetrable, they're not. Just like the gloom that hung over the Jews, the clouds of despair that hover over your life can be chased away, and your life can once again be filled with the sunshine of hope.

 Living Insights STUDY ONE

Walls take many different forms. Some can be physical, others psychological, financial, emotional, spiritual, relational, racial, religious, or marital.

What wall do you find yourself up against?

_____

_____

How do you feel about that wall?

_____

_____

Why does it seems so immovable or impenetrable?

_____

_____

What would God have to do to bring that wall down?

_____

_____

How frequently do you pray for God to tear down that wall?

_____

How fervently?

_____

It didn't make the headlines, but the story behind the toppling of the Berlin wall is a story of prayer. For ten years Christians gathered in a church in Leipzig, East Germany, to pray for the wall to come down. In the final months before the breakdown of the Communist state and the wall's collapse, thousands of Christians met daily to pray for that end, in meetings that spilled over into gigantic demonstrations.[1]

Tennyson was right.

> More things are wrought by prayer
> Than this world dreams of.[2]

1. B. Clayton Bell, Sr., "Revolution by Candlelight," *Christianity Today,* April 23, 1990, p. 16.

2. Alfred, Lord Tennyson, "The Passing of Arthur," *Idylls of the King,* quoted in *Idylls of the King* (and) *Camelot* (New York, N.Y.: Dell Publishing, 1967), p. 155.

Prayer was not only the force behind the wrecking ball that tore down the Berlin wall, it is also the force that can bring down the walls in your life too. If you need some encouragement in this area, read Luke 18:1–8.

 Living Insights

In the seventeenth century Richard Lovelace wrote:

> Stone walls do not a prison make,
>   Nor iron bars a cage.[3]

What Lovelace said is true. Although walls may enclose our body, they cannot imprison our spirit. Unless, of course, we let them. Proverbs warns of the walls that can separate even the closest of relationships.

> A brother offended is harder to be won than a strong
>   city,
> And contentions are like the bars of a castle.
> (18:19)

Look up the following passages to discover how to bring down the walls that may be separating you from others.

Matthew 5:23–24
Ephesians 4:26–27, 29, 31–32

Take the verse that God's Spirit impresses most upon your heart, and make a point to apply it to a relationship where there is a wall. In the space provided, write what you specifically intend to do to help tear down that wall.

_____

_____

_____

_____

Now pick up the phone or take out your pen or go next door or get in the car . . . and do it.

3. *Bartlett's Familiar Quotations,* 14th ed., rev. and enl., ed. Emily Morison Beck (Boston, Mass.: Little, Brown and Co., 1968), p. 358.

Chapter 10

THE LIMITATIONS OF RETALIATION

Esther 9:1–16

Have you ever lost your temper and gone off on a tirade? Have you ever binged while on a diet? Have you ever lost control of your thoughts, where lust or materialism or envy broke out of its harness and ran unbridled through your mind? Have you ever talked too much and later regretted it?

Sure you have. We all have. We've known the pain and regret that come when we let the boundaries of our lives get trampled underfoot.

Today we want to look at something else all of us have trouble keeping on a short leash—retaliation. In Esther 9:1–16, we'll discover the solution to this problem. But before we look at this specific solution, let's briefly examine the problem in general.

The Temptation to Go Too Far

From too many helpings on the all-you-can-eat buffet to exceeding the credit limit on our charge cards, at some time or another we've all gone too far.

We not only go too far in the realms of food and finances, we go too far in the moral realm as well. The saintly apostle Paul himself confessed:

> I don't accomplish the good I set out to do, and the
> evil I don't really want to do I find I am always
> doing. (Rom. 7:19 PHILLIPS)

The problem Paul highlighted resides within us all. It is the universal problem of losing control.

The Key to Holding Back

The answer to our dilemma is as easy to identify as the problem itself. Applying it, however, is a lifetime project. What is the key? Self-control. One authority described it as follows:

> Self-control is managing our attitudes, feelings,
> and actions so they serve our long-term best interests

and those of others. Self-control comes to people who learn discipline and social skills. It increases in those who accept God's grace in their lives and who seek to know and apply divine truth in a disciplined manner.[1]

No matter how discouraged you may be about the lack of this quality in your life, there's encouraging news: Self-control is one of the fruits of the Spirit (Gal. 5:22–23). It can be cultivated—even on the most barren branch.

In Galatians 5:23 the Greek term for *self-control* is a combination of two words that we would translate as *strength* and *in,* meaning "inner strength." It describes those who have mastery over their inner desires, whether those desires are sensual or emotional.

Self-control is the key that unlocks the leg irons of slavery— slavery to those drives and desires that initially seem to be so freeing and fulfilling. Self-control is to a person what brakes are to a car. Without it, a crash is inevitable.

One of the more difficult times of life in which to apply the brakes is when we have the urge to *retaliate.* Webster defines the word: "to repay (as an injury) in kind . . . to return like for like . . . to get revenge."[2]

Retaliation is a warlike response between enemies. But notice how General Douglas MacArthur put the brakes on that response once the war between the United States and Japan was over. After World War II, MacArthur modeled great self-control in helping the Japanese rebuild both their country and their dignity. He could have taken his heel and ground it in Japanese soil in revenge for Pearl Harbor. But he chose instead to rebuild.

Joseph showed similar restraint when he had been mistreated and abandoned by his brothers. The cistern and prison he was thrown into could have become seething caldrons of bitterness and resentment. And when he ascended to Pharaoh's court as the second most powerful man in Egypt, he could have deployed a thousand chariots to trample his brothers in the dust. But he didn't. Instead, he showed great self-control and blessed them.[3]

---

1. Richard P. Walters, *Counseling for Problems of Self-Control,* Resources for Christian Counseling, ed. Gary R. Collins (Waco, Tex.: Word Books, 1987), vol. 11, p. 17.

2. *Webster's Ninth New Collegiate Dictionary,* see "retaliate."

3. For some examples of people who exhibited great self-control, read about David in 1 Samuel 24:1–15 and 26:1–20, and about Jesus in Matthew 26:62–63 and 27:12–14.

This same quality of self-control is illustrated beautifully in our passage for today—Esther 9:1–16.

The Jews Who Were Freed in Persia

Up to this point in the drama, we have seen God change the heart of a king, which resulted in a change of personnel in the palace. Now we see God pulling the strings to intervene in the fate of the Jewish population living in the Medo-Persian Empire.

Through the edict that Mordecai penned and stamped with the king's signet ring, God gave the Jews the legal right to defend themselves. He allowed them to retaliate and plunder anyone who would attack them (8:11, 13).

Yet in their defense they demonstrated remarkable restraint regarding their enemies' families and possessions. Read the account in chapter 9, verses 1–16.

> Now in the twelfth month (that is, the month Adar), on the thirteenth day when the king's command and edict were about to be executed, on the day when the enemies of the Jews hoped to gain the mastery over them, it was turned to the contrary so that the Jews themselves gained the mastery over those who hated them. The Jews assembled in their cities throughout all the provinces of King Ahasuerus to lay hands on those who sought their harm; and no one could stand before them, for the dread of them had fallen on all the peoples. Even all the princes of the provinces, the satraps, the governors, and those who were doing the king's business assisted the Jews, because the dread of Mordecai had fallen on them. Indeed, Mordecai was great in the king's house, and his fame spread throughout all the provinces; for the man Mordecai became greater and greater. Thus the Jews struck all their enemies with the sword, killing and destroying; and they did what they pleased to those who hated them. And in Susa the capital the Jews killed and destroyed five hundred men, and Parshandatha, Dalphon, Aspatha, Poratha, Adalia, Aridatha, Parmashta, Arisai, Aridai, and Vaizatha, the ten sons of Haman the son of Hammedatha, the Jews' enemy; but they did not lay their hands on the plunder.

On that day the number of those who were killed in Susa the capital was reported to the king. And the king said to Queen Esther, "The Jews have killed and destroyed five hundred men and the ten sons of Haman in Susa the capital. What then have they done in the rest of the king's provinces! Now what is your petition? It shall even be granted you. And what is your further request? It shall also be done." Then said Esther, "If it pleases the king, let tomorrow also be granted to the Jews who are in Susa to do according to the edict of today; and let Haman's ten sons[4] be hanged on the gallows." So the king commanded that it should be done so; and an edict was issued in Susa, and Haman's ten sons were hanged. And the Jews who were in Susa assembled also on the fourteenth day of the month Adar and killed three hundred men in Susa, but they did not lay their hands on the plunder.

Now the rest of the Jews who were in the king's provinces assembled, to defend their lives and rid themselves of their enemies, and kill 75,000 of those who hated them; but they did not lay their hands on the plunder.

The Jews were given the legal sanction to utterly destroy their enemies, down to the women and children (8:11). They were even given the right to pillage and plunder the material possessions. But notice their restraint. Nowhere in verses 1–16 of chapter 9 are women and children mentioned as part of the retaliation—only the men. Also, three times we are told that "they did not lay their hands on the plunder" (vv. 10, 15, 16).

The temptation to go too far must have been great, but the Jews resisted. They pulled in the reins rather than let revenge run through the streets, wild and unrestrained.

Human nature tends to do just the opposite. If the offender strikes, the offended strikes back. But if that cycle is ever to be broken, self-control must intervene and gain mastery over vengeance.

---

4. Esther was referring here to the *bodies* of Haman's sons, who had been killed earlier that day.

The Christian Who Is Free Today

When you're tempted to take matters into your own hands, to strike back, to get even, there are a few things you should remember.

First, *remember that, as a Christian, you are to be different from the world.*

> Do not be conformed to this world, but be transformed by the renewing of your mind, that you may prove what the will of God is, that which is good and acceptable and perfect. (Rom. 12:2)

Don't be conformed. Don't let the world squeeze you into its mold. The world's way is to get back. Christ's way is to get us back together (see Matt. 5:38–48).

Second, *remember that, as a Christian, you are a member of a family.*

> For through the grace given to me I say to every man among you not to think more highly of himself than he ought to think; but to think so as to have sound judgment, as God has allotted to each a measure of faith. For just as we have many members in one body and all the members do not have the same function, so we, who are many, are one body in Christ, and individually members one of another. (Rom. 12:3–5)

As a member of a body, your role is not to take charge but to take directions. It is the head's role to give orders, and the head is the Lord Jesus (see also 1 Cor. 12:12–27, Eph. 4:11–16).

Third, *remember that, as a Christian, the Lord is your defender.*

> Never pay back evil for evil to anyone. Respect what is right in the sight of all men. If possible, so far as it depends on you, be at peace with all men. Never take your own revenge, beloved, but leave room for the wrath of God, for it is written, "Vengeance is Mine, I will repay," says the Lord. "But if your enemy is hungry, feed him, and if he is thirsty, give him a drink; for in so doing you will heap burning coals upon his head." Do not be overcome by evil, but overcome evil with good. (Rom. 12:17–21)

Restrain yourself when it comes to revenge. The high road of life is not the road of retaliation. It is the road of forgiveness—the road that Jesus traveled when He went to the cross.

Christ also suffered for you, leaving you an example for you to follow in His steps, who committed no sin, nor was any deceit found in His mouth; and while being reviled, He did not revile in return; while suffering, He uttered no threats, but kept entrusting Himself to Him who judges righteously. (1 Pet. 2:21b–23)

 ## *Living Insights*

Let's explore this whole area of self-control a little further.

Do you struggle with self-control in all areas of your life or just in certain areas?

_____

What areas of your life most frequently get out of control?

_____

_____

_____

Look up the passages that speak to those areas you have a hard time taming.

Your Tongue	Proverbs 17:27–28; James 3:2–18; Ephesians 4:25, 29
Your Thoughts	Matthew 5:19, Proverbs 4:23, Philippians 4:8
Your Time	Ephesians 5:15–17, 1 Thessalonians 5:1–11, 1 Peter 1:17, Psalm 90:12
Your Temper	James 1:19–20; Ephesians 4:26–27, 31–32

Which passage offers the most helpful advice for what you're struggling with now?

_____

Write this passage on a three-by-five-inch card. Take it with you wherever you go. Read it over and over again until it becomes central to your thinking.

Retaliation, though sanctioned in the Old Covenant, is denounced in the New Covenant (Matt. 5:38–42). Jesus taught this both by precept and by example. To see how thoroughly Jesus lived the message He proclaimed, read Matthew 26:47–68 and 27:11–54. Jot down several instances in these passages where Jesus could have retaliated but didn't.

1. _____

2. _____

3. _____

4. _____

5. _____

6. _____

Give three reasons why Jesus didn't retaliate.

(Isa. 53:7) _____

(1 Pet. 2:21) _____

(1 Pet. 2:23b) _____

What positive things happened because Jesus didn't retaliate on the cross?

(Luke 23:39–43) _____

(Luke 23:46–47) _____

What can we learn from Jesus' example on the cross that will help us in our relationships with others (compare Luke 23:33–37 with 1 Pet. 3:8–9)?

_____

_____

Is there someone who has hurt you? Do you find yourself reliving that scene of hurt in your mind and then retaliating, either verbally or physically? Instead of filling your hands with stones, won't you fold them in prayer (Matt. 5:43–44)?

Chapter 11

AFTER THE ACHE, CELEBRATE!

Esther 9:17–32

T oo often we look at life as a drudgery to be endured rather than a dance to be enjoyed. It seems as if it's easier for us to enter into the eulogies at a wake than the excitement at a wedding, to suffer the aches and pains of life than to celebrate the fun and games. Chuck Swindoll's sister, Luci, writes:

> The highest and most desirable state of the soul is to praise God in celebration for being alive. Without perks our lives are easily lost in the world of money, machines, anxieties, or inertia. Our poor, splendid souls! How they fight for food! They have forgotten how to celebrate. They have forgotten how to request little perks. Our hurried, stressful, busy lives are unquestionably the most dangerous enemy of celebrating life itself. Somehow, we must learn how to achieve momentary slowdowns, and request from God a heightened awareness of the conception that life is a happy thing, a festival to be enjoyed rather than a drudgery to be endured. Life is *full* of perks if we train our souls to perceive them, ". . . a thousand tiny things from which one can weave a bright necklace of little pleasures for one's life."[1]

So true, isn't it? But have you ever thought about *why* we tend to be uncomfortable with life's little pleasures? Why we seem more comfortable with lamentation than with celebration? Maybe the reason is because we focus on the past with a sigh.

Looking Over the Past with a Sigh

When we walk down memory lane, our thoughts tend to travel down four well-trodden paths. Those paths circumscribe certain

1. Luci Swindoll, *You Bring the Confetti* (Waco, Tex.: Word Books, 1986), p. 13.

people, events, circumstances, and decisions. And sometimes when we travel down those melancholy paths, we do so with a heavy sigh.

People

Unfortunately, the people we remember most are often the ones who've hurt us rather than the ones who've helped us, the insensitive rather than the inspirational. For the Jews living in Persia at the time of Esther, Haman was the person they would have remembered most. And they would have sighed.

Events

When we look back at events, our minds tend to catalog catastrophes rather than celebrations. We remember with clarity the *Titanic*, Vietnam, Watergate, the space shuttle disaster. But weddings and births and so many Christmases tend to blur around the edges. We remember the date of the last earthquake, tornado, or hurricane but forget the dates of our children's spiritual birthdays. The same was true in Esther's day. The Jews would have looked back to the insidious edict and diabolical plot to exterminate them. And they would have sighed.

Circumstances

Our reminiscences also tend to cluster around certain circumstances. Often those circumstances are wringing wet with blood, sweat, and tears. From divorce to the Great Depression, the memories we hang out to dry are dripping with hardship. The clotheslines in Esther's day were no different. The Jews would have remembered the hardship of living on borrowed time . . . slated for destruction, doomed to die. And they would have sighed.

Decisions

All of us have made wrong decisions in our lives. And many of us are still making monthly payments on those decisions. The bills that come due arrive in the form of shame, guilt, remorse. The accounting was no different in Esther's day. Esther could have regretted her hesitation. Mordecai could have regretted some of the things he said. Certainly Haman, had he repented and been pardoned, would have felt remorse over his decision to kill the Jews. And they all would have sighed.

The whole point of this meandering trip back in time is this: *Anyone who focuses on the past, and keeps focusing on the past, will tend to ache rather than celebrate.*

Fourteen words in Scripture reveal the secret of celebration: "forgetting what lies behind and reaching forward to what lies ahead, I press on . . ." (Phil. 3:13b–14a).

This is the real theme of Esther—not heartache or holocaust. The story of Esther explains how one of the major celebrations in the Jewish calendar, the Feast of Purim, got started. With that in mind, turn your attention to Esther 9, a classic illustration of "forgetting what lies behind and reaching forward to what lies ahead, I press on . . ."

Acknowledging the Present with a Celebration

Before we dig into chapter 9, however, let's leaf back a few pages to chapter 3, where we'll discover the origin of this celebration's name.

> Therefore Haman sought to destroy all the Jews, the people of Mordecai, who were throughout the whole kingdom of Ahasuerus.
>
> In the first month, which is the month Nisan, in the twelfth year of King Ahasuerus, Pur, that is the lot, was cast before Haman from day to day and from month to month, until the twelfth month, that is the month Adar. (vv. 6b–7)

The word *Pur* is an ancient word for "lot," similar in concept to our dice.[2] Haman cast these lots to determine what day would be most auspicious for the Jews' destruction.

The date that came up was the thirteenth day of the twelfth month; that is, the month of Adar. But the gears of the universe are not driven by lottery. They're driven by love. And God's love for the Jewish people ground Haman's plans to a halt. In chapter 9, we find that this day of doom was turned to a day of triumph for the Jews. And when the dust had settled and their destiny was safeguarded, a celebration was called for.

> This was done on the thirteenth day of the month Adar, and on the fourteenth day they rested and made it a day of feasting and rejoicing. But the Jews who were in Susa assembled on the thirteenth and

2. The plural form of the word is *purim* (compare Esther 9:24 with 26). In English, we make our nouns plural by adding s or es. In Hebrew, they pluralize their nouns by adding *im*. For instance, two words depicting angels are *cherub* and *seraph*. Their plurals are *cherubim* and *seraphim*.

the fourteenth of the same month, and they rested
on the fifteenth day and made it a day of feasting
and rejoicing. Therefore the Jews of the rural areas,
who live in the rural towns, make the fourteenth
day of the month Adar a holiday for rejoicing and
feasting and sending portions of food to one another.
(9:17–19)

What appeared to be a time of extermination turned into a time
of celebration. And it was even named after the very thing that
had first appeared as its death knell: Purim. This feast was a festive
occasion. It was much like our own day of Thanksgiving when the
Pilgrims feasted, giving thanks to God for bringing them safely to
the shores of New England and through the rigors of a harsh winter.

This groundswell of celebration came from the Jewish people,
but it was Mordecai who made it official.

Then Mordecai recorded these events, and he
sent letters to all the Jews who were in all the provinces of King Ahasuerus, both near and far, obliging
them to celebrate the fourteenth day of the month
Adar, and the fifteenth day of the same month,
annually, because on those days the Jews rid themselves of their enemies, and it was a month which
was turned for them from sorrow into gladness and
from mourning into a holiday; that they should make
them days of feasting and rejoicing and sending portions of food to one another and gifts to the poor.
Thus the Jews undertook what they had started to
do, and what Mordecai had written to them. For
Haman the son of Hammedatha, the Agagite, the
adversary of all the Jews, had schemed against the
Jews to destroy them, and had cast Pur, that is the
lot, to disturb them and destroy them. But when it
came to the king's attention, he commanded by letter that his wicked scheme which he had devised
against the Jews, should return on his own head,
and that he and his sons should be hanged on the
gallows. Therefore they called these days Purim after
the name of Pur. And because of the instructions in
this letter, both what they had seen in this regard and
what had happened to them, the Jews established

and made a custom for themselves, and for their descendants, and for all those who allied themselves with them, so that they should not fail to celebrate these two days according to their regulation, and according to their appointed time annually. So these days were to be remembered and celebrated throughout every generation, every family, every province, and every city; and these days of Purim were not to fail from among the Jews, or their memory fade from their descendants. (vv. 20–28)

Just as Jews treasure the ceremonies that bring their past to life, so many Americans treasure Washington, D.C., with its national monuments. Our capital is replete with testimonies to the past, like the Washington Monument and the Lincoln Memorial. The masoned stones and chiseled marble give us places where we can read, remember, and reflect. They give the past perspective and significance. And they turn our sighs into smiles of gratitude.

Facing the Future with a Reminder

The establishment of Purim as a perennial custom takes place in verses 29–32.

> Then Queen Esther, daughter of Abihail, with Mordecai the Jew, wrote with full authority to confirm this second letter about Purim. And he sent letters to all the Jews, to the 127 provinces of the kingdom of Ahasuerus, namely, words of peace and truth, to establish these days of Purim at their appointed times, just as Mordecai the Jew and Queen Esther had established for them, and just as they had established for themselves and for their descendants with instructions for their times of fasting and their lamentations. And the command of Esther established these customs for Purim, and it was written in the book.

To this day, Purim is celebrated every year among the Jewish people. In fact, when Jews gather to hear the reading of the Book of Esther, they participate in the story by booing and hissing every time Haman's name is read and cheering whenever Mordecai's name is mentioned.

Isn't that great! Instead of looking back with a heavy sigh or a saddened heart, the Jews treat Purim as a time of fun and feasting and giving gifts.

What does all this say to us today? When most of us think back on the past, our thoughts are tinged with remorse and disappointment. Thumbing through the photo albums of our mind, the details of the past may fade around the edges, while the mistakes we made stand out in sharp relief. In photo after photo we relive those mistakes—mistakes involving people, events, circumstances, and decisions. But those photos should not discourage us. As we look at ourselves today, we should be encouraged that we're different people than we were back then. We've changed. We've grown. We've learned from our mistakes—hopefully.

Many of us, however, don't look through our mental photo albums that way. We groan and moan over what we've wasted, over this done or not done, over things said or unsaid. But before the pity party goes too far, remember: Unending remorse and shame never made anyone better or brought anyone to maturity.

If the past makes you squirm in your pew, let us give you two pieces of advice. One is a suggestion. The other is a warning.

The suggestion is this: *Raise up a mental memorial to turn your sadness into celebration.* A story about a small town in Alabama illustrates the point. One year, the farmers of the area were anticipating a bumper crop of cotton. But then the boll weevil invaded and destroyed the economy in that small rural town. Not to be defeated, one of the farmers got the idea of planting peanuts instead, a crop that the boll weevil won't touch. The idea caught on and, before long, the economy recovered. The town later came to be known as Enterprise, Alabama. And do you know what they did? They raised a monument to the boll weevil! It's there to this day. Isn't that great?

On the heels of that suggestion comes a warning: *Don't turn your memorial into a shrine.* The memorial is merely a reminder. It isn't an end in itself, but a means of turning our thoughts toward the good that the mental monument represents.

An example of a monument turned to a shrine is found in 2 Kings 18:4. The bronze serpent that God used to bring healing to any Israelite who had been snakebitten (see Num. 21:4–9) had been preserved as a memorial, but it later became revered as a shrine, and the Israelites even burned incense to it.

So remember, after the ache—celebrate! But don't let the celebration become an end in itself. Like the celebration of the Lord's Supper, it should be a memorial—not a shrine.

Living Insights

When we look back on the past, we tend to focus on certain people, events, circumstances, and decisions that have impacted our lives. Reflect a few moments on your past, and jot down the things that come to mind in these categories.

People

_____

_____

_____

_____

Events

_____

_____

_____

_____

Circumstances

_____

_____

_____

_____

Decisions

_____

_____

_____

_____

Do you look back on those things with a sigh in your heart? Or with a song?

All of us have skeletons in our closets that rattle in shamed testimony against our past. But those memories are not there to haunt us. They are there to help us—help us learn, understand, forgive, love, do what's right, make restitution if necessary, and trust God for strength and for healing.

When God looks at our lives, He looks at them through the clean lenses of forgiveness. Take David, for example. He was a great king, but he fell into adultery and committed murder (2 Sam. 11). Yet the New Testament calls him a man after God's heart (Acts 13:22) and places him in the Hall of Faith in Hebrews 11 (vv. 32–34). Why? Look at Psalm 51 and you'll see.

David looked back on his past with shame and remorse. Indeed, it *was* a shameful and remorseful past. But David didn't spend the rest of his life cowering inside, crippled by guilt. He did something positive about it. He confessed the sins of his past and accepted God's forgiveness (compare 2 Sam. 12:13 with Ps. 51).

If things from your past come back to point an incriminating finger at you, won't you take them to the Lord and deal with them once and for all? Here are some passages that should encourage you: 1 John 1:9, Psalm 103:8–14, Isaiah 1:18.

 ## *Living Insights* STUDY TWO

Now take one negative memory from each category and turn it into something positive. Out of the rubble of regret, build a monument to God's grace in your life. Describe the negative memory and explain how God has used it for good in your life (Rom. 8:28).

The Rubble of Regret	A Monument of God's Grace
A Person	

An Event

| | |
| | |

A Circumstance

| | |
| | |

A Decision

| | |
| | |

Now take a few minutes to pray, scaling every step in that monument with praise for what God has done—and is doing—in your life.

Chapter 12

In the End, God Wins

Esther 10:1–3

One of the reasons it is possible to go on in spite of struggles and disappointments and heartaches is because we know that in the end, God wins.

Before we get to that triumphant ending, however, we may have to plod through some difficult chapters in our own lives. Chapters where the plot is convoluted. Where pleasure comes only in short sentences. And where pain often forms rambling paragraphs that go on, page after page.

But though the syntax of suffering may grate against our earthly ears, and though the vocabulary of heaven may sometimes be beyond our understanding, the story of life does come together in the end. As God's children, we will indeed live happily ever after.

No matter what tragedies we have had to endure, God will triumph over those tragedies in the end.

The Book of Esther stands on history's shelf like a condensed version of life itself. Though the fate of God's people hung precariously in the balance, in the end God triumphed over the impending tragedy.

A Few Scenes of the End, ahead of Time

To some, all this talk about God winning in the end sounds like fairy-tale thinking. But it is not a pie-in-the-sky, by-and-by type of hope. It is a hope grounded in the truth of Scripture.

> "And He shall wipe away every tear from their eyes; and there shall no longer be any death; there shall no longer be any mourning, or crying, or pain; the first things have passed away." (Rev. 21:4; see also John 14:1–3, Rom. 8:18, 2 Cor. 4:16–18, 2 Tim. 4:7–8)

Heaven will be a paradise illumined by the glory of God, where joy will echo through the corridors of the Father's house. Sin, in all its twisted and grotesque forms, will be forever barred from our eternal estate.

Due to the absence of sin, there will be holiness. Without pain and suffering, there will be perfection. With the final defeat of

Satan, there will be relief and peace. With our new natures and glorified bodies, there will be unity and harmony. With the glory of God radiating resplendently throughout heaven, there will no longer be a need for lesser luminaries like the sun and moon. And with death defeated, immortality will reign. God will be "all in all" (see 1 Cor. 15:22–28).

This sovereign assurance of a happy ending prepares us for the closing chapter in the ancient story of Esther.

A Final Glimpse at the Story, after the Fact

The final chapter in Esther functions like an epilogue, enshrining the hero in an encapsulated tribute.

> Now King Ahasuerus laid a tribute on the land and on the coastlands of the sea. And all the accomplishments of his authority and strength, and the full account of the greatness of Mordecai, to which the king advanced him, are they not written in the Book of the Chronicles of the Kings of Media and Persia? For Mordecai the Jew was second only to King Ahasuerus and great among the Jews, and in favor with the multitude of his kinsmen, one who sought the good of his people and one who spoke for the welfare of his whole nation. (Esther 10:1–3)

The story ends with the same king, the same kingdom, the same country, the same realm of authority, and the same manner of ruling. But unlike the beginning of the story, there has been a major change around the throne. Mordecai has replaced Haman. The presence of evil and corruption and wicked plans is out. Wholeness, peace, and greatness are in.

The last verse informs us that Mordecai has been promoted to second in command and explains why. First, he was "great among the Jews." Second, he was "in favor with the multitude of his kinsmen." Third, he "sought the good of his people." And fourth, he "spoke for the welfare of his whole nation."

Mordecai's promotion was unprecedented in Medo-Persia. He was a Jew in a Gentile country, a country where the Jews had originally come as captives. A comparison of verses 1 and 3 reveals the stark contrast. Verse 1 simply mentions King Ahasuerus, without reference to his race. Verse 3 reads, "Mordecai *the Jew.*"

Why the emphasis on Mordecai's racial origin? Because it was so surprising to see a Jew in such a high political position within a Gentile kingdom. And it could only have happened because God was in charge.

From this small chapter, three potent principles emerge.

Principle one: *When God wins, the people He uses are often unexpected.* Who would have guessed that the one-time gatekeeper would be described the way he is in verse 2? Mordecai's promotion from such humble beginnings is reminiscent of David's ascent from shepherd to king (see Ps. 78:70–72).

In using the most unlikely of people to bring about His victory, God brings into sharp relief the greatness of His sovereign power. For example, He took an eighty-year-old Jew with a criminal record and through him—not a thirty-year-old West Point wiz—pulled off the Exodus.

The list of unlikely recruits goes on and on. Who would have used a harlot to hide Jewish spies? Who would have used a rebel prophet to spearhead an evangelistic crusade in Nineveh? Who would have used a Pharisee and a persecutor of Christians to pen most of the New Testament and to plant churches? Or who would have used a deserter as the foundational rock upon which to build the early church?

Principle two: *When God wins, the qualities He upholds are usually unpretentious.* When the curtain falls on the last scene in the story of Esther, it comes down on a man who stands centerstage in the drama but who bears the marks of true humility. Look at how he is described: "in favor with the multitude of his kinsmen" and one who "sought the good of his people."

The impression you get of Mordecai is that he shied away from the spotlight. He worked behind the scenes, and he did so for the welfare of others. What a beautiful, flesh-and-blood incarnation of the truth found in Philippians 2:3–4.

> Do nothing from selfishness or empty conceit, but with humility of mind let each of you regard one another as more important than himself; do not merely look out for your own personal interests, but also for the interests of others.

Nothing is more Godlike than occupying one's space in lowliness of mind and true servanthood. It is the hallmark of Christ's character (see Matt. 20:28, Luke 22:24–27, John 13:1–15, Phil. 2:5–8).

Principle three: *When God wins, the message He honors most often is universal.* God honors those who have vision, who look beyond themselves to look out for others. The last clause about Mordecai in Esther 10:3 reads literally: "one who spoke for the *peace*[1] of the whole nation."

Mordecai's world was prodigious rather than parochial. It was vast, not limited by the sidewalks and street corners of his own neighborhood. His concern was for the entire nation, not just his own immediate family and close circle of intimate friends.

The largeness of Mordecai's heart reflects God's heart for the world. His desire is for people of *every* tribe, *every* tongue, and *every* nation to know His peace (see Phil. 2:9–11, 1 Tim. 2:4).

Unfortunately, like Haman, our twentieth-century world doesn't honor these principles; it doesn't think like this at all. Which creates a struggle between those who would follow God's principles and those who would oppose them.

A Futile Struggle with God's Plan, Now and Then

Why does our twentieth-century world struggle against God's principles? Three reasons stand out.

When the world selects its major players, the criteria are much different. The chosen ones are sharp, capable, impressive, and strong. They look and sound right and fit the mold of the successful. Because this selection process is so pervasive, it's important to remember: God's choices are often unexpected (1 Sam. 16:7).

When the world looks for qualities that will get a big job done, the externals get the nod. Those who are dressed for success, those with personality and pizzazz are usually the ones given the next rung up on the corporate ladder. But before you take that next step, remember: God upholds the unpretentious and humble (James 4:6).

When the world arranges its priorities, first and foremost it looks out for number one. The heart of the world is self—self-protection, self-promotion, and self-absorption. But don't let the egocentric universe exert any gravitational pull on you. Remember: God's concern is universal. His message reaches out to the whole world (Luke 2:8–10, 29–32).

---

1. The Hebrew word is *shalom*. It encompasses the ideas of security and material blessings.

A Fulfilling Hope for the Christian, in God's Time

All of this is reminiscent of something that happened in a small hamlet outside Jerusalem, in Bethlehem. It was here that God chose to enter the human race. And the vehicle through which He chose to arrive? A young Jewish girl who got pregnant out of wedlock and who became the scandal of Nazareth.

You'd have thought God would have come to Jerusalem through the loins of royalty. But He didn't. He came unexpectedly—in His time and in His way.

And you'd have thought that the birth would have taken place in the imperial palace or at some sprawling estate, crawling with servants. But it didn't. There was not even room in a common inn. The Son of God was born in a barn and cradled in a feeding trough that was cushioned with straw.

And to whom did that little one come? Simply to Mary and Joseph? To His Nazarene neighborhood? No. "God so loved *the world*, that He gave His only begotten Son . . ." (John 3:16a, emphasis added). And those who believe "have eternal life" (v. 16b).

So in the end, not only does God win, but we do too!

In the end of the Book of Esther, God's people emerged triumphant over the forces that sought to exterminate them. It is a story full of twists and turns, heroes and villains. It is a story full of intrigue and political power plays. But most of all, it is a story of God's providential care—and of a woman who was willing to put her life on the line for her people.

 Living Insights

No matter how long the tunnel or how dark, it's easier to keep moving ahead with hope if we know there's light at the end. In his book *Where Is God When It Hurts?* Philip Yancey gives us some illuminating words for times when that tunnel seems too dark, too narrow, and too long for us to carry on.

> [God] has allied Himself with the poor and suffering, establishing a kingdom tilted in their favor, which the rich and powerful often shun.
>
> He has promised supernatural strength to nourish our spirit, even if our physical suffering goes unrelieved.

He has joined us. He has hurt and bled and cried and suffered. He has dignified for all time those who suffer by sharing their pain.

He is with us now, ministering to us through His Spirit and through members of His body who are commissioned to bear us up and relieve our suffering for the sake of the head.

He is waiting, gathering the armies of good. One day He will unleash them. The world will see one last explosion of pain before the full victory is ushered in. Then, He will create for us a new, incredible world. And pain shall be no more.[2]

From the above quote and from Hebrews 4:15 and 5:7–8, how does the Incarnation—God becoming human—help in our suffering?

_____

_____

_____

_____

Yancey says God "is waiting, gathering the armies of good." As members of that army, how can we fight the world's influences (see Rom. 12:2)?

_____

_____

_____

How can we triumph in that battle with the world (see 1 John 5:4–5)?

_____

_____

_____

_____

2. Philip Yancey, *Where Is God When It Hurts?* (Grand Rapids, Mich.: Zondervan Publishing House, 1977), pp. 182–83.

Living Insights

The Book of Esther is a poignant study of the silent government of God, referred to theologically as *providence*. The *New Dictionary of Theology* gives us a good working definition of this doctrine.

> Providence is the beneficent outworking of God's sovereignty whereby all events are directed and dis-posed to bring about those purposes of glory and good for which the universe was made.[3]

Let's search the Scripture to find out what we can about the extent of God's providence.

Scripture	Extent of God's Providence
Psalm 103:19	
Ephesians 1:11	
Psalm 104	
Matthew 10:29	
Matthew 10:30	
Job 12:23	
Psalm 139:16	
Galatians 1:15–16	
Psalm 121	

Now look up Romans 8:28–30 to see what is taught about God's providence in the life of the believer.

Is the promise, "God causes all things to work together for good," universally applicable? Support your answer from the context.

_____

_____

_____

_____

3. *New Dictionary of Theology,* ed. Sinclair B. Ferguson, David F. Wright, and J. I. Packer (Downers Grove, Ill.: InterVarsity Press, 1988), see "Providence."

Does this verse mean that everything that happens to us is good?

_____

How can all things work together *for* good in our lives?

_____

_____

From this passage, what is the ultimate good that our lives are moving toward?

_____

_____

How might this conflict with our idea of what's good for us?[4]

_____

_____

Describe a past event or series of events in which you could clearly see the hand of God working things together for good in your life.

_____

_____

_____

_____

_____

_____

_____

_____

_____

_____

4. For a vivid illustration of this conflict, see the chapter "The Obstinate Toy Soldiers" in C. S. Lewis' book *Mere Christianity*.

Describe how you think His hand is moving in your life now.

BOOKS FOR PROBING FURTHER

The Book of Esther is like a prism. Hold it up to the light and you can see a rainbow of brightly colored subjects. The spectrum ranges from the courage of the queen to the silence of heaven; from principles of communication in marriage to the providence of God.

Should you want to study any of these subjects in greater detail, we have provided a list of books for your further reading.

Courage

Andrew, Brother, with Dave and Neta Jackson. *A Time for Heroes.* Ann Arbor, Mich.: Servant Publications, Vine Books, 1988. The Book of Esther drips with the heroism of Esther and Mordecai— ordinary people who changed the course of history. We live today in an age that has been depleted of its natural resources of heroes, yet Brother Andrew asserts that every Christian is called to greatness. He takes us on a tour of the Scriptures, pointing out heroes from the past along the way. By highlighting these men and women, the author shows how God crafts heroes from the ordinary mud and mortar of humanity.

Johnston, Jon. *Courage.* Wheaton, Ill.: SP Publications, Victor Books, 1990. When Esther stood up for her people, she did so at a risk to her own life. Her courage, however, averted a holocaust and forever enshrined her as a heroine of the Jewish people. But this unlikely queen of Medo-Persia was not a bold, crusading firebrand. She was demure and soft-spoken. In this well-written book, the author calls believers to face their fears and demonstrate the courage of their convictions—just as Esther did.

The Silence of Heaven

Jacobs, Joy. *When God Seems Far Away.* Wheaton, Ill.: Tyndale House Publishers, 1988. Joy Jacobs has experienced distance from God, distance often caused by her own fear, guilt, inadequacy, anger, and doubt. She has also bridged that distance and learned to embrace God. Through a reflective study of the Hebrew names for God, she shows how we, too, can bridge that distance.

Marshall, Catherine. *Light in My Darkest Night.* Old Tappan, N.J.: Fleming H. Revell Co., Chosen Books, 1989. A series of devastating events that culminated in the death of her baby granddaughter threw Catherine Marshall's faith into a tailspin. She cried out to God in her agony and in her anger, yet for all her tears, she received back only the hollow echo of her own prayers bouncing off heaven's gate. In this honest and intimate book, the author offers hope to anyone who has ever experienced spiritual silence.

Patterson, Ben. *Waiting.* Downers Grove, Ill.: InterVarsity Press, 1989. Subtitled *Finding Hope When God Seems Silent,* this book deals with the emotions experienced when we feel God has placed our lives on hold. The author explores the mystery of waiting and the wisdom of God in making us wait. Exploring the lives of two men who had to wait, Job and Abraham, Patterson unearths two golden treasures required for successful waiting—humility and hope.

The Providence of God

Berkouwer, G. C. *The Providence of God.* Translated by Lewis B. Smedes. Grand Rapids, Mich.: William B. Eerdmans Publishing Co., 1952. This theological text is the second volume in the series Studies in Dogmatics. With careful scholarship and sparkling clarity, this theologian conducts a thorough study of how God rules and watches over His creation. The author examines biblical texts, church history, and contemporary scholars to construct a compelling case for God's providence, which pervades the Book of Esther.

Principles of Communication in Marriage

Groom, Nancy. *Married without Masks.* Colorado Springs, Colo.: NavPress, 1989. Esther lived in a day when the woman's role was rigidly defined and husbands ruled autocratically in the marriage relationship. When Esther spoke out against the edict her husband had decreed, she stepped from behind the mask that her society placed over women and expressed herself with transparency and conviction. In this excellent look at marriage, the author discusses the biblical relationship between submission and authority, and shows us all how to be honest, open, and married without masks.

Smalley, Gary, and John Trent. *The Language of Love*. Pomona, Calif.: Focus on the Family Publishing, 1988. Probably the greatest area in which people have trouble communicating is that of their own marriage. Sensitive issues are often shelved for "a more convenient time" that never comes, or else they are suppressed altogether. Esther learned how to broach touchy subjects with her husband. So can you. In this excellent book, the authors show how to develop the communication skills you need to share those feelings that are so sensitive and difficult to express.

Insight for Living
Cassette Tapes
ESTHER
A WOMAN FOR SUCH A TIME AS THIS

At first brush, the story of Esther appears to be simply a Cinderella tale of a young Jewish girl who finds favor with a king, becomes his queen, and bravely speaks up at the right time to save her people from annihilation. It is all of this . . . but so much more! For this is as much a story of God's sovereignty as it is of the people He loves so much . . . the story of His omnipotent orchestration of human affairs for His glory and the good of His children. So, as you peer into the pages of Esther's life, marvel at the wonder of it. Then ponder Mordecai's words—"Who knows whether you have not attained royalty for such a time as this?"—and imagine their implication for your own life.

			Calif.*	U.S.	B.C.*	Canada*
EST	CS	Cassette series, includes album cover	$36.66	$34.50	$49.44	$46.81
EST	1–6	Individual cassettes, include messages A and B	5.31	5.00	7.18	6.79

These prices are subject to change without notice.

EST 1-A: *God's Invisible Providence*—Survey of Esther
     B: *"There She Goes . . . Miss Persia!"*—Esther 1:1–2:7

EST 2-A: *Queenlike Qualities of a Lovely Lady*—Esther 2:8–20
     B: *An Evil Interlude*—Esther 2:21–3:15

EST 3-A: *Thinking, Saying, and Doing What's Right—Regardless—*Esther 4
     B: *The Beginning of a Collision Course*—Esther 5

EST 4-A: *Turnabout Is Fair Play*—Esther 6
     B: *Ultimate Poetic Justice*—Esther 7

EST 5-A: *And the Wall Came Tumbling Down*—Esther 8
     B: *The Limitations of Retaliation*—Esther 9:1–16

EST 6-A: *After the Ache, Celebrate!*—Esther 9:17–32
     B: *In the End, God Wins*—Esther 10:1–3

*These prices already include the following charges: for delivery in **California,** 6¼% sales tax; **Canada,** 7% postage and handling; **British Columbia,** 6% British Columbia sales tax and 7% postage and handling.

How to Order by Mail

Simply mark on the order form whether you want the series or individual tapes. Mail the form with your payment to the appropriate address listed below. We will process your order as promptly as we can.

United States: Mail your order to the Sales Department at Insight for Living, Post Office Box 4444, Fullerton, California 92634. If you wish your order to be shipped first-class for faster delivery, add 10 percent of the total order amount (not including California sales tax). Otherwise, please allow four to six weeks for delivery by fourth-class mail. We accept personal checks, money orders, Visa, or MasterCard in payment for materials. Unfortunately, we are unable to offer invoicing or COD orders.

Canada: Mail your order to Insight for Living Ministries, Post Office Box 2510, Vancouver, British Columbia V6B 3W7. Please add 7 percent of your total order for first-class postage and allow approximately four weeks for delivery. Our listeners in British Columbia must also add a 6 percent sales tax to the total of all tape orders (not including postage). We accept personal checks, money orders, Visa, or MasterCard in payment for materials. Unfortunately, we are unable to offer invoicing or COD orders.

Australia, New Zealand, or Papua New Guinea: Mail your order to Insight for Living, Inc., GPO Box 2823 EE, Melbourne, Victoria 3001, Australia. Please allow six to ten weeks for delivery by surface mail. If you would like your order sent airmail, the delivery time may be reduced. Whether you choose surface or airmail, postage costs must be added to the amount of purchase and included with your order. Please use the chart that follows to determine correct postage. Due to fluctuating currency rates, we can accept only personal checks made payable in U.S. funds, international money orders, Visa, or MasterCard in payment for materials.

Overseas: Other overseas residents should contact our United States office. Please allow six to ten weeks for delivery by surface mail. If you would like your order sent airmail, the delivery time may be reduced. Whether you choose surface or airmail, postage costs must be added to the amount of purchase and included with your order. Please use the chart that follows to determine correct postage. Due to fluctuating currency rates, we can accept only personal checks made payable in U.S. funds, international money orders, Visa, or MasterCard in payment for materials.

Type of Postage	Postage Cost
Surface	10% of total order
Airmail	25% of total order

For Faster Service, Order by Telephone

To purchase using Visa or MasterCard, you are welcome to use our **toll-free** numbers between the hours of 8:30 A.M. and 4:00 P.M., Pacific time, Monday through Friday. The number to call from anywhere in the United States is **1-800-772-8888.** To order from Canada, call our Vancouver office at **1-800-663-7639.** Vancouver residents should call (604) 272-5811. Telephone orders from overseas are handled through our Sales Department at (714) 870-9161. We are unable to accept collect calls.

Our Guarantee

Our cassettes are guaranteed for ninety days against faulty performance or breakage due to a defect in the tape. For best results, please be sure your tape recorder is in good operating condition and is cleaned regularly.

Note: To cover processing and handling, there is a $10 fee for *any* returned check.

Order Form

EST CS represents the entire *Esther* series in a special album cover, while EST 1–6 are the individual tapes included in the series.

Tapes	Calif.*	Unit Price U.S.	B.C.*	Canada*	Quantity	Amount
EST CS	$36.66	$34.50	$49.44	$46.81		$
EST 1	5.31	5.00	7.18	6.79		
EST 2	5.31	5.00	7.18	6.79		
EST 3	5.31	5.00	7.18	6.79		
EST 4	5.31	5.00	7.18	6.79		
EST 5	5.31	5.00	7.18	6.79		
EST 6	5.31	5.00	7.18	6.79		
					Subtotal	
					Overseas Residents *Pay U.S. price plus 10% surface postage or 25% airmail. Also, see "How to Order by Mail."*	
					U.S. First-Class Shipping *For faster delivery, add 10% for postage and handling.*	
					Gift to Insight for Living *Tax-deductible in the United States and Canada.*	
					Total Amount Due *Please do not send cash.*	$

If there is a balance: ☐ apply it as a donation ☐ please refund

*These prices already include applicable taxes and shipping costs.

Form of payment:

☐ Check or money order made payable to Insight for Living

☐ Credit card (circle one): Visa MasterCard

Card Number _____ Expiration Date _____

Signature _____
We cannot process your credit card purchase without your signature.

Name _____

Address _____

City _____

State/Province_____ Zip/Postal Code _____

Country _____

Telephone (_____) _____ Radio Station ____ ____ ____ ____
If questions arise concerning your order, we may need to contact you.

Mail this order form to the Sales Department at one of these addresses:
Insight for Living, Post Office Box 4444, Fullerton, CA 92634
Insight for Living Ministries, Post Office Box 2510, Vancouver, BC, Canada V6B 3W7
Insight for Living, Inc., GPO Box 2823 EE, Melbourne, VIC 3001, Australia

Order Form

EST CS represents the entire *Esther* series in a special album cover, while EST 1–6 are the individual tapes included in the series.

Tapes	Calif.*	Unit Price U.S.	B.C.*	Canada*	Quantity	Amount
EST CS	$36.66	$34.50	$49.44	$46.81		$
EST 1	5.31	5.00	7.18	6.79		
EST 2	5.31	5.00	7.18	6.79		
EST 3	5.31	5.00	7.18	6.79		
EST 4	5.31	5.00	7.18	6.79		
EST 5	5.31	5.00	7.18	6.79		
EST 6	5.31	5.00	7.18	6.79		
				Subtotal		
				Overseas Residents *Pay U.S. price plus 10% surface postage or 25% airmail. Also, see "How to Order by Mail."*		
				U.S. First-Class Shipping *For faster delivery, add 10% for postage and handling.*		
				Gift to Insight for Living *Tax-deductible in the United States and Canada.*		
				Total Amount Due *Please do not send cash.*		$

If there is a balance: ☐ apply it as a donation ☐ please refund

*These prices already include applicable taxes and shipping costs.

Form of payment:

☐ Check or money order made payable to Insight for Living

☐ Credit card (circle one): Visa MasterCard

Card Number _____ Expiration Date _____

Signature _____
We cannot process your credit card purchase without your signature.

Name _____

Address _____

City _____

State/Province_____ Zip/Postal Code _____

Country _____

Telephone ( ) _____ Radio Station ____ ____ ____ ____
If questions arise concerning your order, we may need to contact you.

Mail this order form to the Sales Department at one of these addresses:
Insight for Living, Post Office Box 4444, Fullerton, CA 92634
Insight for Living Ministries, Post Office Box 2510, Vancouver, BC, Canada V6B 3W7
Insight for Living, Inc., GPO Box 2823 EE, Melbourne, VIC 3001, Australia